Power-Up College English
<Basic>

パワーアップ・イングリッシュ
<基礎編>

JACET リスニング研究会

NAN'UN-DO

このテキストの音声を無料で視聴（ストリーミング）・ダウンロードできます。自習用音声としてご活用ください。
以下のサイトにアクセスしてテキスト番号で検索してください。

https://nanun-do.com　テキスト番号 [**498053**]

※ 無線 LAN（WiFi）に接続してのご利用を推奨いたします。

※ 音声ダウンロードは Zip ファイルでの提供になります。お使いの機器によっては別途ソフトウェア（アプリケーション）の導入が必要となります。

※ Power-Up College English <Basic> 音声ダウンロードページは以下の QR コードからもご利用になれます。

Power-Up College English <Basic>
パワーアップ・イングリッシュ〈基礎編〉

by
JACET SIG on Listening

©2019 All Rights Reserved.
No part of this publication may be reproduced or transmitted in any form or by any means without permission from the authors and Nan'un-do Co., Ltd.

はじめに

　本書『パワーアップ・イングリッシュ＜基礎編＞』は、ロングセラーを続けているパワーアップシリーズの姉妹編となる Nan'un-do Semester Series *Power-Up College English* 第1作目にあたり、大学生としてぜひ身につけておきたい英語力（聴解力、読解力、会話力、文法力、および作文力）の基礎を積極的に学習できるよう配慮された、まさにオールラウンドな英語教材です。

本書の特徴は次の3つです。
(1) トピックは、身近な話題「趣味」「スポーツ」「旅行」から、大学生として理解を深めておきたい話題「教育」「科学」「社会・国際問題」に至るまで多岐にわたり、リスニング、リーディング、及びライティングの3つのセクションではユニットごとにトピックに関連性を持たせています。従って、学習者は学びやすく、興味・関心を抱いて問題に取り組むことができます。
(2) スピーキングセクションでは、日常生活における様々な場面において想定される、"決まり文句"を伴う対話をとりあげました。無造作に棒読みをしたり、一途に暗記するのではなく、語句の発音や強勢の位置を意識して、正しいイントネーションを伴った発話を求めています。また、英語の語順どおりに並べ替えた日本語を見て、それを英語に置き換えることで、自然と英文が頭の中に構築され、その英文が抵抗なく自分の言葉として発話されることを狙っています。学習の際、日本語を見ながら何度も英語音声を聞き、発話した後で、学習者自らがサイトトランスレーション（後ろから前に戻らずに、文を文頭から区切って訳す方法）を行えば、自然なスピーキングへの橋渡しとなることでしょう。
(3) ライティングセクションでは、長めの和文英訳は難しいことを考慮し、Exercise 1、2 においては、部分英作文の手法を取り入れています。また、Exercise 3 においては、同じ Unit の Reading Passage の一部（太字部分）を参考にして和文英訳をするという方式を採択しました。英語のアウトプットは例文・連語・構文等のインプット（暗記）に始まるという自明な理由によるものです。実際の作業は、主として数語を入れ替えるという単純なものですが、結果だけを見れば、10語を超える英文を記述することになり、「英語を書いた」という達成感が得られ、英作文への自信を深めることにもなります。

　刊行にあたり、南雲堂編集部の加藤 敦氏、英文校閲などを担当していただきました Michael P. Critchley 氏に大変お世話になりました。ここに深く感謝の意を表します。

2018年8月
執筆者一同

本書の構成と学び方

本書は全14ユニット（各ユニット4ページ仕立て）の構成で、半期用に対応できるように編集されています。各ユニットは5セクションから成り立ち、各ユニットのフォーマットを統一したことで、学習計画が立てやすく、授業展開もスムーズに進められます。

● Listening Section（1ページ）

◆ Listening Tips
リスニング力の向上に役立つコツやヒントを用例付きで紹介しています。

◆ Exercise 1
「絵」について、3つの短い描写文を聞き、正しく叙述している文を選びます。

◆ Exercise 2
発話とそれに対する3つの応答を聞き、発話に最もふさわしい応答を1つ選びます。

◆ Exercise 3
70語程度の英文を聞き、その内容について記載された2つの設問に答えます。

● Reading Section（1ページ半）

◆ Words & Phrases
Reading Passage より抜粋された語（句）に一致する日本語訳を選択します。

◆ Reading Passage
各ユニットのトピックに関連した題材を取り上げて、250語程度で書かれた英文です。

◆ Exercise 1
Main Idea を問う問題を含め、空所補充の問題形式で本文の内容理解を確認します。

◆ Exercise 2
本文の内容について記述された英文の真偽を問う問題で、内容の理解度を確かめます。

● Speaking Section（半ページ）

◆ Exercise 1
英語の強く発音するところを黒く塗り、英語の正しいリズム感を理論立てて学びます。

◆ Exercise 2
英語の語順通りに並べ替えた日本語を見て、英語を聞き話すことでスピーキング力の基礎を養います。

◆ Exercise 3
短い対話形式で発話を楽しみながら、日常生活における感情表現を自然と身につけます。

● Grammar Section（半ページ）

◆ Exercise 1
標記の文法項目について、空所に入る適切な語句を選択肢の中から選びます。

◆ Exercise 2
標記の文法項目に基づいた空所補充問題で、文法力の基礎を習得するのに効果的です。

● Writing Section（半ページ）

◆ Exercise 1
語順に注意して、与えられた語を正しく並べ替えて英文を完成させます。

◆ Exercise 2
与えられた日本文に合うように、適語を補って英文を完成させます。

◆ Exercise 3
Reading Passage の一部（太字部分）を参考に、和文英訳により作文力の向上を図ります。

● Appendix
文法項目が要領よくまとめてあります。予習や復習など、自主学習にも役立ちます。

CONTENTS

Unit 1 Hobby / Entertainment 9
- **L** 英文のリズム 1   **R** Growing Vegetables at Home「野菜づくりのすすめ」
- **S**「感謝」の表現   **G** 5文型   **W**「趣味／娯楽」に関わる表現

Unit 2 Travel/Transportation 13
- **L** 英文のリズム 2   **R** The Fastest Train in the World「世界最速列車」
- **S**「喜び」の表現   **G** 現在形・過去形   **W**「旅行・乗り物」に関わる表現

Unit 3 Sports 17
- **L** グループ単位の聞き方   **R** American Football「アメリカンフットボール」
- **S**「誘い」の表現   **G** 進行形・完了形   **W**「スポーツ」に関わる表現

Unit 4 Culture 21
- **L** 強形・弱形   **R** American Holidays「アメリカの祝日」
- **S**「賞賛」の表現   **G** 助動詞   **W**「文化」に関わる表現

Unit 5 Health 25
- **L** イントネーション   **R** Healthy Diet, *Washoku*「健康食—和食」
- **S**「依頼」の表現   **G** 受動態   **W**「健康」に関わる表現

Unit 6 Career 29
- **L** 強調   **R** Job Hunting「就職活動」
- **S**「詫び」の表現   **G** 不定詞・動名詞   **W**「就職活動」に関わる表現

Unit 7 Education 33
- **L** 短縮形の発音   **R** Education System「日米の教育システム」
- **S**「断り」の表現   **G** 名詞・代名詞   **W**「教育」に関わる表現

Unit 8 Science 37
- **L** 消える音 1   **R** Search for Life on Other Planets「地球外生命の探査」
- **S**「激励」の表現   **G** 形容詞・副詞   **W**「科学」に関わる表現

Unit 9 **Business** 41
　　L 消える音2　R Financial Support of the People's Bank 「貧困者救済への銀行の試み」　S 「賛同」の表現　G 前置詞　W 「ビジネス」に関わる表現

Unit 10 **Social Issues** 45
　　L 消える音3　R Passive Smoking 「受動喫煙」
　　S 「反対」の表現　G 接続詞　W 「社会問題」に関わる表現

Unit 11 **Natural Disasters** 49
　　L つながる音1　R Hope for the Best and Prepare for the Worst 「備えあれば憂いなし」　S 「承諾」の表現　G 比較　W 「災害」に関わる表現

Unit 12 **International Issues** 53
　　L つながる音2　R Fairtrade Products 「発展途上国への支援」
　　S 「忠告」の表現　G 関係代名詞　W 「国際問題」に関わる表現

Unit 13 **Technology** 57
　　L アメリカ英語の発音　R Hopes and Concerns about Robot Technology 「ロボットへの期待と不安」　S 「感想」の表現　G 関係副詞　W 「科学技術」に関わる表現

Unit 14 **Music** 61
　　L イギリス英語の発音　R The Power of Music 「音楽に宿るパワー」
　　S 「別れ」の表現　G 仮定法　W 「音楽」に関わる表現

Appendix　Unit別 Grammar Points の解説 65

Unit 1 Hobby / Entertainment

● Listening Section ●

Listening Tips

英文のリズム 1 — 強く発音されるところはどこ？—

英語の文は強弱リズムで、通常、単語の種類が強弱に影響します。
強く発音（●表示）→ 内容語（名詞、be 動詞以外の動詞、形容詞、副詞、数詞、疑問詞など）
弱く発音（○表示）→ 機能語（be 動詞、助動詞、冠詞、代名詞、前置詞、接続詞など）

Growing vegetables is a popular hobby.　　You can start if you have a small sunny space.
● ● ○ ○ ●　●　　　　　○ ○ ● ○ ● ○ ● ● ●

Exercise 1 Listen to the CD and choose the statement that best describes the picture.

1. (a)　(b)　(c)　　　　　2. (a)　(b)　(c)

Exercise 2 Listen to the CD and choose the best response.

1. (a)　(b)　(c)　　　2. (a)　(b)　(c)　　　3. (a)　(b)　(c)

Exercise 3 Listen to the CD and choose the best answer.

1. What is essential for cycling?

    (a) Drinks and towels

    (b) A map and a helmet

    (c) Sneakers and skirts

2. How should you carry necessaries for cycling?

    (a) In pockets

    (b) In a big bag

    (c) In a backpack

Unit 1

● Reading Section ●

Growing Vegetables at Home

Words & Phrases 次の語句の意味を選びなさい。

1. rewarding ( ) 2. encourage ( ) 3. container ( ) 4. chemical ( )
5. water ( ) 6. headache ( ) 7. restore ( ) 8. slug ( )
9. effective ( ) 10. leftover ( )

(a) 栽培容器　(b) ナメクジ　(c) 水を撒く　(d) 飲み残しの　(e) 効果的な
(f) 化学物質　(g) 悩みの種　(h) 回復する　(i) 奨励する　(j) やりがいのある

次の文を読んで、後の設問に答えなさい。

Reading Passage

　Growing vegetables is a popular hobby. It is both interesting and rewarding. How about giving it a try at your own home? You can start if you have a small, sunny space around your house. It's okay to use planters on the veranda.

5　There are some advantages in growing vegetables at home. One is that it's a lot of fun to see small vegetable plants growing bigger day by day until they come into bloom and then bear fruit. Another is that you can safely eat fresh vegetables grown without chemicals.

　However, you have to take good care of your vegetables if you expect to have a good harvest. When you water them in summer, you should wear long pants and
10　a long-sleeved shirt to avoid mosquito bites. You will find yourself covered with sweat, but you can't complain about it, because you will enjoy a good harvest of fresh vegetables in autumn.

　Another headache is to protect plants from the attack of harmful insects or worms. You should know that the damaged leaves will never be restored. The
15　worst enemy in your garden may be slugs because they are active at night and hide somewhere in the daytime. An effective way of getting rid of them is to make use of leftover beer. You put a plate with some beer in it near your vegetable plants in the evening. You will find a lot of drowned slugs in the plate the following morning. Believe it or not, slugs like beer.

20　Health matters above all else. **Fresh and safe vegetables help you stay healthy.** Why don't you grow vegetables in your garden?

(272 words)

give ～ a try ～をやってみる　planter プラスチック製の長方形の容器で、底部に排水用の穴あり。　advantage メリット　come into bloom 開花する　bear fruit 実をつける　water 水撒きをする　sweat [swet] 汗　harmful insects or worms 害虫（バッタや毛虫など）　Believe it or not まさかと思うでしょうが　plate 小皿状の容器　matter 重要である

Hobby / Entertainment

Exercise 1   ( ) 内に入る最も適切な語句を選び、文を完成させなさい。

1. This passage focuses mainly on how to (   ) vegetables at home.
   (a) eat   (b) grow   (c) cook
2. You can make use of leftover (   ) to get rid of slugs from a vegetable garden.
   (a) beer   (b) juice   (c) soda
3. Home-grown vegetables are recommended because they are (   ).
   (a) fresh and safe   (b) fresh and less expensive   (c) safe and tasty

Exercise 2   次の各文が本文の内容に合っていれば T(True)、合っていなければ F(False) と書きなさい。

_____ 1. A vegetable garden must be made at the corner of a house.
_____ 2. If you want to have a good harvest, you have to water vegetables every day.
_____ 3. All leftover drinks are useful to get rid of slugs.

● Speaking Section ●
「感謝」の表現

Exercise 1   強く発音するところの○を黒く塗り、CD を聴いて確認しなさい。次に、英語を見ながら CD を聴いてリピートしなさい。最後に、シャドーイングしなさい。

1. A: Here's a birthday present for you. It's a smartphone case. I hope you like it.

   B: I've been wanting one for a long time. **Thank you very much**.

2. A: What's up? You seem to be troubled. Can I help you?

   B: Really? **That's very kind of you**. I've got to finish this assignment by next Sunday.

Exercise 2   次の日本語を見ながら、シャドーイングしなさい。

1. A: これ / 誕生日プレゼント / 君に // スマホケースだよ // いいな / 気に入ってくれたら //
   B: それが欲しかったんだ / ずっと // 有難う //
2. A: どうかしたの // みたいだね / 困っている // 手伝おうか //
   B: ほんとうなの // それはご親切にどうも // いけないんだ / 終えないと / この研究課題を / 次の日曜までに //

Exercise 3   上記の日本語を見ながら、次に何も見ないでペアで交互に英語で会話しなさい。

Unit 1

● **Grammar Section** ●

5文型

★ Grammar Points は Appendix (p.65) を参照

Exercise 1 （ ）に入る適切な語句を選び、文型を数字で示しなさい。

1. We (discussed / discussed about) the plans for growing vegetables at home.　　第（ ）文型

2. She seemed (exciting / excited) to have a rich harvest in her garden.　　第（ ）文型

3. I found a lot of slugs (drown / drowned) in a plate the next morning.　　第（ ）文型

Exercise 2 a), b)の2文が同意になるように（ ）内に適切な語を書き入れ、各文の文型を言いなさい。

1. a) Her hobby is reading.　　第（ ）文型
   b) She reads (　　) as a hobby.　　第（ ）文型

2. a) I made my dog a doghouse.　　第（ ）文型
   b) I made a doghouse (　　) my dog.　　第（ ）文型

● **Writing Section** ●

「趣味／娯楽」に関わる表現

Exercise 1 （ ）内の語を並べかえて文を完成させなさい。

1. Mary (up / as / took / a / knitting) hobby.
   Mary _____ hobby.

2. (pastime / fishing / good / is / a) for my father.
   _____ for my father.

Exercise 2 日本文に合うように適当な英語を補って文を完成させなさい。

1. 弟は写真を撮ることに関心があります。
   My brother has an (　　) (　　) (　　) pictures.

2. 妹はピアノを弾くのが上手です。
   My sister is (　　) (　　) (　　) (　　) piano.

Exercise 3 日本文を英語に直しなさい。

新鮮で安全な野菜は健康な生活を送るのに役立ちます。

Unit 2 Travel/Transportation

● Listening Section ●

Listening Tips

英文のリズム２ ― 文単位での強勢はどうなる？―

英文のリズムは強勢が置かれる箇所と弱く発音される箇所から構成されます。○の数に関わらず、●がほぼ等時間隔で現れます。

1. The girl　　reads　　　　　 books.
　　○●　　　　●　　　　　　　●
2. The girl　　has been reading　the book.
　　○●　　　○　○　●　　　　○●

Exercise 1　Listen to the CD and choose the statement that best describes the picture.

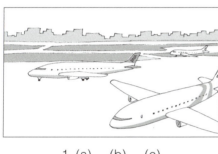

　　1. (a)　(b)　(c)　　　　　　2. (a)　(b)　(c)

Exercise 2　Listen to the CD and choose the best response.

1. (a)　(b)　(c)　　　　2. (a)　(b)　(c)　　　　3. (a)　(b)　(c)

Exercise 3　Listen to the CD and choose the best answer.

1. What are the passengers requested to do in the announcement?

　(a) To fasten their seat belts

　(b) To reserve the flight

　(c) To board the plane

2. How long does it take to fly to Rome?

　(a) 12 hours and 14 minutes

　(b) 12 hours and 40 minutes

　(c) 20 hours and 14 minutes

Unit 2

● Reading Section ●

The Fastest Train in the World

Words & Phrases 次の語句の意味を選びなさい。

1. vehicle ( )   2. compete ( )   3. track ( )   4. operate ( )
5. float ( )   6. friction ( )   7. capacity ( )   8. alternative ( )
9. suspension ( )   10. experience ( )

(a) 乗り物   (b) 運行する   (c) 軌道   (d) 休止   (e) 競争する
(f) 浮揚する   (g) 摩擦   (h) 代わりの   (i) 体験する   (j) 受容力

次の文を読んで、後の設問に答えなさい。

Reading Passage

　Trains are one of the most popular vehicles. Japan, China, and some European countries have been competing hard to make the world's fastest train.

　Japan's new maglev train hit a top speed of 603 km/h and set a world speed record on its test track near Mt. Fuji in April 2015. It is expected that the maglev train will operate at a maximum speed of 505 km/h, while the top operating speed of a Shinkansen train is 320 km/h. Therefore, the maglev train would cover the 286 km between Tokyo and Nagoya in 40 minutes by 2027, and the 438 km between Tokyo and Osaka in 67 minutes by 2045.

　The maglev train uses very strong magnets to force it up off the tracks and move it forward. Japan's maglev train doesn't run on rails. It floats a few inches above the tracks, moving forward without friction, but it uses tires when it runs at low speed or comes to a stop at a station.

　The JR Tokai train company says, "We have decided to develop the maglev service because the Tokaido Shinkansen has reached the limit of its carrying capacity and because we need an alternative route when an earthquake or other disaster causes operating suspensions along the Tokaido Shinkansen."

　The day will come in the near future when passengers can ride on the world's fastest maglev train and experience the thrill of traveling at a much faster speed than a Shinkansen train.

(244 words)

maglev train 磁気浮上式列車（鉄道）、リニアモーターカー。磁石の性質（同極間では反発力、異極間では吸引力が働く）を利用して車両を浮上させて走行する。走行路に非接触のため、高速走行が可能になり、騒音や振動が軽減されるという利点もある。(maglev は magnetic levitation「磁気浮揚」が語源)　　develop the maglev service 磁気浮上式鉄道の事業開発を行う

Travel/Transport

Exercise 1   （　）内に入る最も適切な語句を選び、文を完成させなさい。

1. This passage focuses mainly on (　) of Japan's maglev train.
   (a) the high speed　　(b) the comfortable ride　　(c) the operating cost
2. Japan's maglev train would connect Nagoya and Osaka in (　).
   (a) 37 minutes　　(b) 27 minutes　　(c) 17 minutes
3. Japan's maglev train (　) when it stops at a station.
   (a) uses tires　　(b) runs on rails　　(c) floats a few inches above the tracks

Exercise 2   次の各文が本文の内容に合っていれば T(True)、合っていなければ F(False) と書きなさい。

____ 1. The top operating speed of the maglev train is almost double that of a Shinkansen train.

____ 2. Japan's maglev train is a few inches above the tracks even when it is stopped at a station.

____ 3. The Shinkansen train will no longer operate between Tokyo and Osaka when the maglev train connects the two cities.

● Speaking Section ●
「喜び」の表現

Exercise 1   強く発音するところの○を黒く塗り、CD を聴いて確認しなさい。次に、英語を見ながら CD を聴いてリピートしなさい。最後に、シャドーイングしなさい。

1. A: I hear you received the first prize in the picture contest yesterday.

   B: Yes, I did. I didn't expect any prize, but **I am happy to** win the prize.

2. A: **We are pleased to** know you beat the champion at chess.

   B: Thank you. It's just good luck. I'll try harder next time, too.

Exercise 2   次の日本語を見ながら、シャドーイングしなさい。

1. A: 聞いているよ / 君は取ったんだって / 一等賞を / 写真コンテストで / きのう //
   B: はい、そうだよ // 期待していなかったよ / どのような賞も / でもうれしいよ / 賞がとれて //
2. A: 喜んでいるよ / 知って / 君が勝ったことを / チャンピオンに / チェスにおいて //
   B: 有難う // そのことはまさにまぐれだったんだよ // もっと頑張るよ / 次も //

Exercise 3   上記の日本語を見ながら、次に何も見ないでペアで交互に英語で会話しなさい。

Unit 2

● Grammar Section ●
現在形・過去形

★ Grammar Points は Appendix (p.65) を参照

Exercise 1 （　）に入る適切な語句を選びなさい。

1. She (hurries / hurried) to the station to catch the train last night.
2. Let's go to a picnic in the woods when she (comes / came).
3. Jim (goes / went) for a drive with Jane this coming Sunday.

Exercise 2 （　）内の語を適切な形に直しなさい。

1. Here (come) the bus! Are you ready to get on?
2. The guide showed her a sightseeing map when she (ask) him the way to the temple.
3. Our trip plan will be canceled if it (rain) tomorrow.

● Writing Section ●
「旅行・乗り物」に関わる表現

Exercise 1 （　）内の語を並べかえて文を完成させなさい。

1. She (part / of / thinks / taking / in) the tour in summer.
   She _____ the tour in summer.

2. The subway (minutes / every / during / three / runs) the rush hours.
   The subway _____ the rush hours.

Exercise 2 日本文に合うように適当な英語を補って文を完成させなさい。

1. 外国人観光客にはどうして日本の列車は時間通り走れるのか驚きです。
   It is surprising to foreign tourists how trains in (　　) (　　) (　　) (　　) time.

2. 最寄りの駅まで歩いて時間はどれほどかかりますか。
   How long does (　　) (　　) (　　) (　　) to the nearest station?

Exercise 3 日本文を英語に直しなさい。

近い将来、私たちは新幹線よりはるかに速いスピードで旅行するスリルを体験することでしょう。

_____

Unit 3 Sports

● Listening Section ●

Listening Tips

グループ単位の聞き方 — 文中の区切りはどこ？—

文の構成要素（主語、動詞、目的語や句、節など）はひと息で発音され、意味のまとまり（sense group）と一致します。語順通りに意味のまとまりの単位で聞きましょう。

What I want to write about / is the two beautiful women / who sang a wonderful song /
私が書きたいことは　　　／二人の美しい女性で　　　　／素晴らしい歌を披露しました　／
at the college festival.
それは大学祭でのことでした。

Exercise 1 Listen to the CD and choose the statement that best describes the picture.

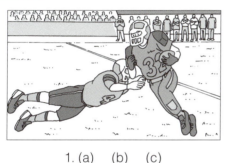

1. (a)   (b)   (c)   2. (a)   (b)   (c)

Exercise 2 Listen to the CD and choose the best response.

1. (a) (b) (c)   2. (a) (b) (c)   3. (a) (b) (c)

Exercise 3 Listen to the CD and choose the best answer.

1. According to the passage, what sport was popular 30 years ago?

    (a) Skiing

    (b) Snowboarding

    (c) Surfing

2. When was snowboarding first included in the Winter Olympics?

    (a) 30 years ago

    (b) In 1998

    (c) In 2004

Unit 3

● Reading Section ●

American Football

Words & Phrases 次の語句の意味を選びなさい。

1. relatively (　)　2. compare (　)　3. spectator (　)　4. complicated (　)
5. offensive (　)　6. attempt (　)　7. gain (　)　8. possession (　)
9. strategy (　)　10. opponent (　)

　(a) 対戦相手　(b) 観客　(c) 複雑な　(d) 努力する　(e) 比較的
　(f) 所持　(g) 獲得する　(h) 攻撃の　(i) 戦略　(j) 比較する

次の文を読んで、後の設問に答えなさい。

Reading Passage

　Have you heard about the Super Bowl? It is the NFL (National Football League) championship game. Tickets to the Super Bowl are very expensive. It sometimes costs more than $10,000 just for one seat. According to a survey by *The Washington Post*, 37% of American people chose American football as their favorite
5　sport to watch, whereas only 11% chose baseball.

　In Japan, the number of American football players is relatively small compared to other sports. However, the number of spectators for the Koshien Bowl, a university championship game for American football, was around 35,000, much larger than that for rugby, which stands at 13,000, or soccer at 5,700 in 2017.

10　Why is American football so popular? It is because fighting for points with well-trained players is quite dynamic. The rules are quite complicated. But the basic rules are as follows. The offensive team tries to advance down the field by carrying or passing the ball, whereas the defensive team attempts to stop the offence's advance by tackling or intercepting passes. The offense must advance at least ten
15　yards in four plays to be given another set of plays, otherwise, the opposing team gains possession of the ball. Players can score 6 points by a touchdown when they advance the ball across the end zone, or 3 points by kicking the football through the goal posts.

　The strategy of American football is important and complicated. Usually,
20　teams have analysts who think of game strategies. Strong teams have more than 100 game plans against each opponent. If you understand the basic rules and strategies, you can surely enjoy the game more.

(272 words)

NFL アメリカ合衆国で最上位に位置するプロフットボールリーグ　　the Koshien Bowl 全日本大学アメリカンフットボール選手権大会の決勝戦のことで、毎年12月の第3日曜日に甲子園球場にて開催　　as follows 次の通り　　intercepting インターセプト（攻撃側がパスしたボールを守備側の選手が反則なしにキャッチすること）　　touchdown タッチダウン（相手のエンドゾーンにボールを持ち込むこと、得点方法の一つ）　　analyst 相手チームのデータを分析し戦略などを考えるスタッフ

Sports

Exercise 1 （　）内に入る最も適切な語句を選び、文を完成させなさい。

1. This passage focuses mainly on how (　) American football is.
   (a) funny   (b) attractive   (c) dangerous
2. The most expensive Super Bowl tickets are sometimes more than (　) just for one seat.
   (a) $1,000   (b) ¥10,000   (c) $10,000
3. If the offense can't advance (　) yards in four plays, it loses possession of the ball.
   (a) four   (b) a hundred   (c) ten

Exercise 2 次の各文が本文の内容に合っていれば T(True)、合っていなければ F(False) と書きなさい。

____ 1. Baseball is the most popular sport to watch in America.
____ 2. The number of spectators for the Koshien Bowl was 13,000 in 2017.
____ 3. Strong teams have more than 100 strategies against each opponent, which are usually created by team analysts.

● Speaking Section ●

「誘い」の表現

Exercise 1 強く発音するところの○を黒く塗り、CD を聴いて確認しなさい。次に、英語を見ながら CD を聴いてリピートしなさい。最後に、シャドーイングしなさい。

A: **We should definitely get together**. Could we meet soon?

B: My schedule is rather tight, but I'd love to, when things settle down.

A: I have two tickets for the ball game on Saturday. **Would you like to come with me?**

B: That'll be great. Where should we meet?

Exercise 2 次の日本語を見ながら、シャドーイングしなさい。

A: 絶対に / 会おうね // 会えるかな / 近いうちに //
B: 私のスケジュールでは / ちょっと厳しい / でもそうしたいね / 落ち着いたら //
A: チケット2枚持ってる / 野球の / 土曜日の // 来たい / 私と一緒に //
B: それはうれしい // どこで / 会おうか //

Exercise 3 上記の日本語を見ながら、次に何も見ないでペアで交互に英語で会話しなさい。

Unit 3

● **Grammar Section** ●

進行形・完了形

★ Grammar Points は Appendix (p.66) を参照

Exercise 1 （　）内に入る適切な語句 Sports を選びなさい。

1. Have you ever (been / gone) to an American football game?
2. I was (playing / played) tennis when you called me.
3. The girl has been learning dance (for / since) five years.

Exercise 2 2文がほぼ同じ意味になるように（　）内に入る適切な語を書き入れなさい。

1. Peter (　　) (　　) (　　) soccer for five years.
   = Peter started playing soccer five years ago and he still plays it.
2. Maki (　　) (　　) watched such an exciting tennis game.
   = This is the first time for Maki to watch such an exciting tennis game.
3. An hour has passed since I started jogging.
   = I have (　　) (　　) for an hour.

● **Writing Section** ●

「スポーツ」に関わる表現

Exercise 1 （　）内の語を並べかえて文を完成させなさい。

1. Have (watched / you / game / an American football / ever) on TV?
   Have _____ on TV?
2. How long (played / you / have / in / basketball) the Japanese League?
   How long _____ the Japanese League?

Exercise 2 日本文に合うように適当な英語を補って文を完成させなさい。

1. お母さんが帰ってくる頃には、テニスの試合は終わっているでしょう。
   The tennis match (　　) (　　) (　　) over by the time my mother comes back.
2. 日本ではアメリカンフットボールの選手の数は増えてきています。
   The number of American football players in Japan (　　) (　　) (　　).

Exercise 3 日本文を英語に直しなさい。

サッカーの作戦は重要で複雑です。

Unit 4 Culture

● Listening Section ●

Listening Tips

強形・弱形 ― at も強く聞こえることがある？―

機能語には、弱く聞こえる場合（弱形）と強く聞こえる場合（強形）があります。
通常、機能語は弱形で発音されますが、文末に置かれる場合や、強調や対比を表す場合は強形になることがあります。

1. Look <u>at</u> the map.（弱形）What are you looking <u>at</u>?（強形）　　　［文末］
2. <u>Can</u> you go there?（弱形）I <u>can</u> go, but I don't want to.（強形）　　　［強調］
3. It is <u>on</u> the desk.（弱形）It is <u>on</u> the desk, not under it.（強形）　　　［対比］

Exercise 1 Listen to the CD and choose the statement that best describes the picture.

1. (a)　(b)　(c)　　　　　　2. (a)　(b)　(c)

Exercise 2 Listen to the CD and choose the best response.

1. (a)　(b)　(c)　　　2. (a)　(b)　(c)　　　3. (a)　(b)　(c)

Exercise 3 Listen to the CD and choose the best answer.

1. What did the speaker tell you to do first?

    (a) Boil some eggs.

    (b) Put stickers on the eggs.

    (c) Choose your favorite food coloring.

2. Which of the following is NOT needed to make Easter eggs?

    (a) Sugar

    (b) Vinegar

    (c) Food coloring

Unit 4

● Reading Section ●

American Holidays

Words & Phrases 次の語句の意味を選びなさい。

1. celebrate (　)　2. tradition (　)　3. boiled (　)　4. dye (　)
5. independence (　)　6. legend (　)　7. spirit (　)　8. wander (　)
9. neighborhood (　)　10. feast (　)

(a) 独立　(b) 霊　(c) 歩き回る　(d) 伝統　(e) 伝説
(f) 染料　(g) ご馳走　(h) 祝う　(i) 近所　(j) ゆでた

次の文を読んで、後の設問に答えなさい。

Reading Passage

　What is your favorite holiday? Every culture has its own events, and people celebrate them with special traditions and meals. Here are four events, one from each season, celebrated in the United States.

　Easter falls in the spring. It celebrates the rebirth of Jesus Christ. Children enjoy Easter egg coloring and an Easter egg hunt. They put boiled eggs into water with dye and make colorful eggs. They also enjoy hunting for eggs the Easter bunny has hidden.

　The Fourth of July is a national holiday in the US. This summer holiday is also known as Independence Day, which commemorates America's independence from Great Britain. People enjoy parades, BBQs, and fireworks on this day.

　In fall, there is Halloween. People carve pumpkins to make jack-o'-lanterns. The tradition goes back to the Irish legend in which a man named Jack becomes an evil spirit and wanders around with a lantern. Although people used turnips for carving a face in to scare the evil spirit away in the past, pumpkins have been used since the tradition came to America. On Halloween night, children put on their favorite costume to go trick-or-treating in the neighborhood to receive candy.

　Christmas is a big event in winter. Colorful decorations are put on a Christmas tree, and presents are put underneath it on Christmas Eve. **Family members get together and have Christmas dinner**. Various dishes, such as roast turkey, ham, pie, fruits and vegetables, are served for the feast. They enjoy the holiday season at the end of the year.

(254 words)

rebirth 復活　　Easter bunny イースター・バニー（復活祭に子どもたちにプレゼントを持ってくるといわれるうさぎ）　　commemorate 祝う　　BBQ バーベキュー　　turnip カブ　　go trick-or-treating ハロウィンに子どもたちが仮装して近所の家々を回り、お菓子をもらうこと

Culture

Exercise 1 （ ）内に入る最も適切な語句を選び、文を完成させなさい。

1. This passage focuses mainly on (　　).
   (a) seasonal events　　(b) American independence　　(c) what children love
2. Children enjoy (　　) for eggs on Easter.
   (a) searching　　(b) praying　　(c) throwing
3. People put colorful (　　) on a Christmas tree.
   (a) decorations　　(b) presents　　(c) costumes

Exercise 2 次の各文が本文の内容に合っていれば T(True)、合っていなければ F(False) と書きなさい。

_____ 1. Holidays are celebrated with special traditions and meals.
_____ 2. Easter celebrates the birth of Jesus Christ.
_____ 3. Great Britain's independence from America is a national holiday in the U.S.

● Speaking Section ●
「賞賛」の表現

Exercise 1 強く発音するところの○を黒く塗り、CD を聴いて確認しなさい。次に、英語を見ながら CD を聴いてリピートしなさい。最後に、シャドーイングしなさい。

1. A: You sure did a great job on that speech. **It was amazing**.

   B: Thank you. I tried my best, but I had butterflies in my stomach.

2. A: **I'm impressed** with your presentation.

   B: Thank you. I had been preparing for a while.

Exercise 2 次の日本語を見ながら、シャドーイングしなさい。

1. A: 本当によくやったね / あのスピーチ // すばらしかったよ //
   B: ありがとう // がんばったんだ / けど緊張したよ //
2. A: 感動したよ / あなたの発表に //
   B: ありがとう // 準備してきたんだ / ここしばらく //

Exercise 3 上記の日本語を見ながら、ペアで交互に英語で会話しなさい。

Unit 4

● Grammar Section ●
助動詞

★ Grammar Points は Appendix (p.66) を参照

Exercise 1 （　）に入る適切な語句を選びなさい。

1. This is very delicious. You (will / should) try some.
2. I'm sorry but I (cannot / do not) come to the party tomorrow because I have to study.
3. "(Must / May) I unwrap the present?" "Of course. Go ahead."

Exercise 2 （　）内に入る語を答えなさい。

1. You (　　　) drive on the right side of the road in America.
2. Come to the party as early as you (　　　).
3. I enjoyed the movie very much. You really (　　　) see it.

● Writing Section ●
「文化」に関わる表現

Exercise 1 （　）内の語を並べかえて文を完成させなさい。

1. You (not / stories / must / ghost / believe).
   You _____.

2. You (offer / to / seat / should / your) the elderly on public transportation.
   You _____ the elderly on public transportation.

Exercise 2 日本文に合うように適当な英語を補って文を完成させなさい。

1. アメリカでは家の中で靴を履いていてもよろしい。
   You (　　) (　　) (　　) (　　) on inside the house in America.

2. 女性に年齢を聞くべきではありません。
   (　　) (　　) (　　) (　　) a woman her age.

Exercise 3 日本文を英語に直しなさい。

日本ではお正月に (at New Year's) 家族が集まっておせち料理 (New Year's food) を食べます。

_____

Unit 5 Health

● Listening Section ●

Listening Tips

イントネーション — 声の上がり、下がりはどうなる？—

英文のイントネーションには、下降調（↘）、上昇調（↗）などのパターンがあります。

1. I went to the festival. (↘)
2. Did you go to the concert? (↗)
3. Where did you go? (↘)
4. Which do you like better, summer (↗) or winter? (↘)

Exercise 1 Listen to the CD and choose the statement that best describes the picture.

1. (a)　(b)　(c)　　　　2. (a)　(b)　(c)

Exercise 2 Listen to the CD and choose the best response.

1. (a)　(b)　(c)　　　2. (a)　(b)　(c)　　　3. (a)　(b)　(c)

Exercise 3 Listen to the CD and choose the best answer.

1. First, what do you put in the rice?

   (a) *Nori*

   (b) Sugar and vinegar

   (c) Tuna and cucumber

2. After putting fillings such as tuna on rice, what will you do with the sushi?

   (a) Cut it into slices.

   (b) Lay a *nori* sheet.

   (c) Roll it up.

Unit 5

● Reading Section ●

Healthy Diet, *Washoku*

Words & Phrases 次の語句の意味を選びなさい。

1. longevity (　)　2. healthy (　)　3. register (　)　4. ingredient (　)
5. soybean (　)　6. balanced (　)　7. nutrient (　)　8. moderation (　)
9. prevent (　)　10. cancer (　)

(a) 材料　(b) 控えめ　(c) 長寿　(d) 栄養素　(e) 防ぐ
(f) 登録する　(g) 癌　(h) 健康によい　(i) バランスのとれた　(j) 大豆

次の文を読んで、後の設問に答えなさい。

Reading Passage

　Japanese people live long. One of the secrets of this longevity is that Japanese food is healthy. *Washoku* was registered as a UNESCO Intangible Cultural Heritage in 2013. One of the reasons for the registration of *washoku* is the attractiveness of its appearance and its pleasant taste. The other reason that we want to focus on here is its healthfulness.

　Washoku uses healthy ingredients, such as *tofu*, *miso*, soy sauce, and *natto*, which are made from soybeans. Moreover, some *washoku* can be part of a *macrobiotic* diet, which means a healthy and balanced diet. It includes vegetables, beans, and whole grains. It has been drawing international attention and been popular among celebrities like Madonna and Tom Cruise.

　As *washoku* is praised as a model for a healthy diet, we can learn a lot from *washoku*. Balance, variety, and moderation are keys to eating healthfully. The first key is balance. Try to eat from each food group: grains, protein foods, fruits, vegetables, and dairy. The second one is food variety. Select as many foods as possible from each food group. Don't choose an orange every time you buy a fruit. By eating many kinds of foods each day, you will get all the nutrients that you need. Lastly, eat food in moderation. Stop eating before you feel full. As the old saying goes, moderate eating keeps the doctor away.

　Healthy eating is one of the best ways to prevent many life-style related diseases, such as cancer and heart disease, and to live a happy and longer life. Get started on healthy eating today!

(262 words)

UNESCO Intangible Cultural Heritage ユネスコ無形文化遺産　　whole grain 全粒穀物（果皮、種皮、胚、などを除去していない穀物・その製品。玄米、発芽玄米、オートミールなど）　　celebrity 著名人　　life-style related diseases 生活習慣病

Health

Exercise 1 （　）内に入る最も適切な語句を選び、文を完成させなさい。

1. This passage focuses mainly on the (　) of *washoku*.
   (a) taste　　(b) appearance　　(c) healthfulness
2. Madonna and Tom Cruise love the *macrobiotic* diet, which is a (　) diet.
   (a) balanced　　(b) colorful　　(c) staple
3. You should stop eating before you feel (　).
   (a) full　　(b) hungry　　(c) good

Exercise 2 次の各文が本文の内容に合っていれば T(True)、合っていなければ F(False) と書きなさい。

____ 1. The ingredients in *washoku* are good for the human body.
____ 2. Eating as much as you like is a good way to live long.
____ 3. Healthy eating can prevent cancer or heart disease.

● Speaking Section ●
「依頼」の表現

Exercise 1 強く発音するところの○を黒く塗り、CD を聴いて確認しなさい。次に、英語を見ながら CD を聴いてリピートしなさい。最後に、シャドーイングしなさい。 🎧 31

1. A: **Excuse me**. **Will you** lend me your textbook? I left mine at home.

   B: Sure. I won't need it till next Friday.

2. A: **Would you mind** help**ing** me to write a paper on a global problem?

   It is difficult for me.

   B: No problem. I'll be free this afternoon.

Exercise 2 次の日本語を見ながら、シャドーイングしなさい。

1. A: ごめん // 貸してもらえる / 教科書を // 私のを置いてきた / 家に //
   B: もちろん // 要らない / 金曜日まで //
2. A: 助けてもらえる / 論文を書くのを / 地球規模の問題について // 難しい / 私にとって //
   B: いいよ // 空いてる / 午後は //

Exercise 3 上記の日本語を見ながら、ペアで交互に英語で会話しなさい。

Unit 5

● **Grammar Section** ●

受動態

★ Grammar Points は Appendix (p.67) を参照

Exercise 1 （ ）に入る適切な語句を選びなさい。

1. My apple was (eating / eaten) by the boy.
2. Fresh food was (given / gave) to the dog by the owner.
3. Bill was (kept healthy / kept be healthy) by the special diet.

Exercise 2 （ ）内に入る語を答えなさい。

1. Tom Cruise wrote this get-well card. = This get-well card was (　　　) by Tom Cruise.
2. They will open the restaurant at five. = The restaurant will (　　　) opened at five.
3. Eating in moderation keeps the doctor away.
   = The doctor (　　　) kept away by moderate eating.

● **Writing Section** ●

「健康」に関わる表現

Exercise 1 （ ）内の語を並べかえて文を完成させなさい。

1. Healthy ingredients　(Japanese / in / are / food / used).
   Healthy ingredients _____.
2. *Tofu* and (made / soybeans / are / *natto* / from).
   Tofu and _____.

Exercise 2 日本文に合うように適当な英語を補って文を完成させなさい。

1. 和食は世界中で称賛されています。
   (　　) (　　) (　　) all over the world.
2. バランスの取れた食物が選ばれなくてはなりません。
   Well-balanced (　　) (　　) (　　) (　　).

Exercise 3 日本文を英語に直しなさい。

健康的な食事は生活習慣病を防ぐ良い方法です。

Unit 6 Career

● Listening Section ●

> **Listening Tips**
>
> 強調 — どこを強調する？—
>
> 伝達したい重要な情報は、ほかの語句よりも強く、長く発音されることがあります。
>
> 1. JOHN bought three books.　　　　　　「誰が」が重要
> 2. John BOUGHT three books.　　　　　　「何をした」が重要
> 3. John bought THREE books.　　　　　　「いくつ買った」が重要
> 4. John bought three BOOKS.　　　　　　「何を買った」が重要

Exercise 1 Listen to the CD and choose the statement that best describes the picture.

1. (a)　(b)　(c)　　　　　　2. (a)　(b)　(c)

Exercise 2 Listen to the CD and choose the best response.

1. (a)　(b)　(c)　　　2. (a)　(b)　(c)　　　3. (a)　(b)　(c)

Exercise 3 Listen to the CD and choose the best answer.

1. What is especially important for job hunting?

    (a) Skills for getting information

    (b) Experience of part-time jobs

    (c) Business suits

2. What communication skill is NOT mentioned?

    (a) Understanding others

    (b) Expressing your ideas

    (c) Non-verbal communication like gestures

Unit 6

● Reading Section ●

Job Hunting

Words & Phrases 次の語句の意味を選びなさい。

1. abolish (　)　2. alumni (　)　3. avoid (　)　4. gauge (　)
5. toughness (　)　6. apply (　)　7. accomplishment (　)
8. frustrating (　)　9. endeavor (　)　10. perseverance (　)

(a) 努力　(b) 評価する　(c) 成果　(d) 挫折感を味わうような　(e) 困難
(f) 忍耐強さ　(g) 避ける　(h) 応募する　(i) 廃止する　(j) 同窓生（複数形）

次の文を読んで、後の設問に答えなさい。

Reading Passage

　The Japan Business Federation has decided to abolish the guidelines for corporate hiring of university students to give flexibility in recruiting.

　In the future, students may be able to start going through various hunting processes anytime, including researching companies, doing internships, alumni
5　visits, attending company seminars, writing applications (*ESs or Entry Sheets* in Japanese), and taking the *SPI (Synthetic Personality Inventory)*.

　Using job-hunting support websites, such as *Mynavi*, *En*, and *Rikunabi*, and **experiencing internships are good ways to learn about the actual jobs** and to avoid mismatches between the company and the student. Companies might
10　give students a group task to gauge their leadership, problem-solving abilities, teamwork abilities, mental toughness, and communication skills in seminars. Abilities to gather information make a big difference in the number of job offers obtained by students.

　The first step in applying for a job is submitting an *ES* to companies. Some
15　students submit more than 100 *ESs* if they haven't decided which type of industry to work in. Their accomplishments, academic achievements, strengths and weaknesses can be explained in the *ESs*.

　After passing the first selection through the *ESs* and *SPI*, interviews can begin. Large companies sometimes hold three or more interviews. Interviewers often
20　ask about applicants' strengths and reasons for application. They sometimes ask such unique questions as "Can you describe an experience in which you got angry recently in a funny way?" This type of question could indirectly reveal the person's way of thinking about problem solving.

　Finally, students offered the position are informed by e-mail, telephone, or
25　even during the final interview. Job hunting can be a long, tough, and frustrating endeavor. Students surely develop their perseverance and become more mature through this experience.

(283 words)

The Japan Business Federation 日本経団連　　flexibility 柔軟性　　*ES* エントリーシート（書類選考で用いられる応募書類）　　*SPI (Synthetic Personality Inventory)* 日本の適性検査　　indirectly reveal 間接的に明らかにする

Exercise 1 （　）内に入る最も適切な語句を選び、文を完成させなさい。

1. This passage is mainly about job hunting (   ).
   (a) failures　　　(b) processes　　　(c) interviews
2. According to the passage, companies might give students (   ) to evaluate their leadership, communication skills, and so on.
   (a) a group task　　　(b) e-mail　　　(c) *ESs*
3. Applicants' strengths and the (   ) for application are often asked in the job interviews.
   (a) occupation　　　(b) fee　　　(c) reason

Exercise 2 次の各文が本文の内容に合っていればT(True)、合っていなければF(False)と書きなさい。

____ 1. In the future, students will have to start going through various hunting processes all at once.
____ 2. Submitting an *ES* to companies is the first step in applying for a job.
____ 3. The promises of post-graduation employment are informed only by e-mail.

● Speaking Section ●
「詫び」の表現

Exercise 1 強く発音するところの○を黒く塗り、CDを聴いて確認しなさい。次に、英語を見ながらCDを聴いてリピートしなさい。最後に、シャドーイングしなさい。

1. A: **I apologize for** being late.
   ○　○　　　○　○

   B: No problem. Did you run into any trouble?
   ○　○　　○　○　○　○　　○

2. A: Could you turn down the music?
   　　○　　○　○　○　　　○　○

   B: **I'm so sorry**. I didn't realize someone was there.
   ○　○　○　　○　○　　○　　○　　　　○　○

Exercise 2 次の日本語を見ながら、シャドーイングしなさい。

1. A: すみません / 遅くなってしまって //
   B: いいですよ // どうかしたのですか //
2. A: 音量をさげてくれない / 音楽の //
   B: 本当にごめん // 気がつかなかったの / そこに誰かがいるなんて //

Exercise 3 上記の日本語を見ながら、ペアで交互に英語で会話しなさい。

Unit 6

● **Grammar Section** ●

不定詞・動名詞

★ Grammar Points は Appendix (p.67) を参照

Exercise 1 （ ）内から適切な語句を選びなさい。

1. I am looking forward to (hearing / hear) from the company.
2. It is very kind (of / for) you to teach me how to write a résumé.
3. How about (to write / writing) *Entry Sheets* together?

Exercise 2 2文がほぼ同じ意味になるように（ ）内に入る適切な語を書き入れなさい。

1. She is a good job hunter.= She is good at (　　　) (　　　).

2. It might be difficult to obtain job positions when you don't attend companies' seminars.
   = It might be difficult to obtain job positions (　　　) (　　　) companies' seminars.

3. The students are so busy that they can't prepare enough for job hunting.
   = The students are (　　　) busy (　　　) prepare enough for job hunting.

● **Writing Section** ●

「就職活動」に関わる表現

Exercise 1 （ ）内の語を並べかえて文を完成させなさい。

1. Indirect questions are often asked to (of / thinking / evaluate / your / way).
   Indirect questions are often asked to _____.

2. My sister is (to / not / old / enough / apply) for this part-time job.
   My sister is _____ for this part-time job.

Exercise 2 日本文に合うように適当な英語を補って文を完成させなさい。

1. このエントリーシートの書き方を教えてください。
   Please teach me (　　　) (　　　) (　　　) this *Entry Sheet*.

2. この会社説明会に参加するのはどうですか。
   (　　　) (　　　) (　　　) this company seminar?

Exercise 3 日本文を英語に直しなさい。

インターンシップに参加することは、実際の仕事を知る上で良い方法です。

Unit 7 Education

● **Listening Section** ●

Listening Tips

短縮形の発音 — he's は、he is それとも he has ?—

話し言葉では be 動詞、助動詞 have, has, had, will, would などは、主語と結びついて短縮されることがあります。なかでも、is と has や had と would などは短縮形が全く同じ音になるので注意が必要です。短縮形の語末は聞こえにくくなることがあります。

1. He is a student. → He's a student.   [be 動詞の短縮]
2. He has gone. → He's gone.   [助動詞の短縮]
3. I would like to go. → I'd like to go.   [助動詞の短縮]

Exercise 1 Listen to the CD and choose the statement that best describes the picture.

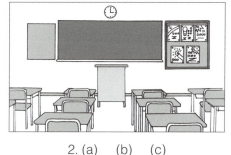

1. (a)   (b)   (c)   2. (a)   (b)   (c)

Exercise 2 Listen to the CD and choose the best response.

1. (a)   (b)   (c)   2. (a)   (b)   (c)   3. (a)   (b)   (c)

Exercise 3 Listen to the CD and choose the best answer.

1. What is this announcement about?
   (a) Changes in the library's open hours
   (b) Changes in the library's open days
   (c) The usual closing time of the library

2. How long is the schedule change for?
   (a) From 8 a.m. to 10:00 p.m.
   (b) Three hours
   (c) Two days

Unit 7

● Reading Section ●

Education System

Words & Phrases 次の語句の意味を選びなさい。

1. reflect ( )   2. compulsory ( )   3. approved ( )   4. quantity ( )
5. vary ( )   6. kindergarten ( )   7. district ( )
8. skip ( )   9. achievement ( )   10. outstanding ( )

(a) 異なる   (b) 成績   (c) 承認された   (d) 幼稚園   (e) 義務的な
(f) 極めて優れた   (g) 地区   (h) 量   (i) 反映する   (j) 飛び級をする

次の文を読んで、後の設問に答えなさい。

Reading Passage

　Education systems differ from country to country and might reflect a country's societal values. Let's have a look at some differences between Japanese and American education.

5 　In Japan, compulsory education starts from the first grade of elementary school and continues through the third year of junior high school. The curriculum is decided by the government, and subjects are taught using government-approved textbooks. Textbooks are provided for free. Children in compulsory education advance in school year no matter what their grades are. This system allows all children to receive equal access to and quantity of education.

10 　In the US, however, formal education varies depending on the state. Mandatory education is usually from kindergarten to grade 12 (K-12). Students go to school from around the age of five to eighteen. Each school district decides its curriculum and textbooks, which students borrow from the school to study. Even in their compulsory education, children might fail the school year and have 15 to repeat it. **Some students might be able to skip some school years if their achievement has been good enough.** There are gifted or talented programs for students with outstanding skills. They take different classes from others and receive more challenging assignments. These programs can provide education that can meet the different needs of each student.

20 　Which of these systems is more appealing to you? Each has its strengths and weaknesses and might reflect societal values; the collectivism of Japanese society and the individualism of American society.

(244 words)

mandatory 義務的な　　gifted and talented program 優秀な生徒のための特別なカリキュラム　　meet the different needs 異なるニーズに応える　　collectivism 集団主義　　individualism 個人主義

Education

Exercise 1 （　）内に入る最も適切な語句を選び、文を完成させなさい。

1. This passage focuses mainly on (　).
   (a) the education systems of America and Japan　　(b) gifted students
   (c) students' educational achievement

2. Each school (　) decides the curriculum and textbooks in the US.
   (a) teacher　　(b) principal　　(c) district

3. Gifted or talented programs are for students with (　) skills.
   (a) lower　　(b) higher　　(c) average

Exercise 2 次の各文が本文の内容に合っていれば T(True)、合っていなければ F(False) と書きなさい。

____ 1. In Japan compulsory education lasts nine years.

____ 2. Japanese education gives all students the same gifted program.

____ 3. Every child in America has to go to school for sixteen years.

● Speaking Section ●

「断り」の表現

Exercise 1 強く発音するところの○を黒く塗り、CD を聴いて確認しなさい。次に、英語を見ながら CD を聴いてリピートしなさい。最後に、シャドーイングしなさい。

1. A: We have a school play tomorrow evening. Can you come and see it?

   B: **I'd love to, but** I have a prior engagement.

   I'll definitely come next time, so please let me know.

2. A: Will you help me with this project? It's due tomorrow, and I'm running out of time.

   B: **I'm sorry, but** I have to finish this paper tonight. I have to hand this in tomorrow, too.

Exercise 2 次の日本語を見ながら、シャドーイングしなさい。

1. A: 学校の劇があるの / 明日の夕方 // 観に来てくれる //

   B: 是非行きたいんだけど / 先約があるの // 次は絶対に行くから / 知らせてね //

2. A: 手伝ってくれる / この課題 // 明日が期限で / 時間がないの //

   B: ごめんね / このレポートを終えなければならないの / 今晩 // 提出しなくてはならないの / 私も明日 //

Exercise 3 上記の日本語を見ながら、ペアで交互に英語で会話しなさい。

Unit 7

● **Grammar Section** ●

名詞・代名詞

★ Grammar Points は Appendix (p.68) を参照

Exercise 1 （ ）に入る適切な語句を選びなさい。

1. The professor gave us (an / some) advice about the research.
2. We have to get (many / a lot of) data for the paper.
3. I want to buy some new (furniture / furnitures) for my dorm room.

Exercise 2 （ ）内に入る語を答えなさい。

1. He had two (   ) (   ) coffee to stay awake for studying.
2. I don't need these textbooks anymore. You can have (   ).
3. I lost my ruler. I have to buy a new (   ).

● **Writing Section** ●

「教育」に関わる表現

Exercise 1 （ ）内の語を並べかえて文を完成させなさい。

1. (many / you / how / classes / are) taking this semester?
   _____ taking this semester?

2. You have to (elementary / years / six / attend / of) school.
   You have to _____ school.

Exercise 2 日本文に合うように適当な英語を補って文を完成させなさい。

1. 経済学の授業で2つ宿題 (assignment) が出ました。
   We've received (   ) (   ) (   ) our economics class.

2. この授業で不合格だったら、もう一度、来年取らなければなりません。
   If you fail this course this year, you have to (   ) (   ) (   ) next year.

Exercise 3 日本文を英語に直しなさい。

彼はもし成績がよければ、その学校に入ることができるかもしれません。

_____

Unit 8 Science

● **Listening Section** ●

Listening Tips

消える音 1 — Let's stop. はどう聞こえる？—

[p] [t] [k] [b] [d] [g] などは、語末、句末、文末では聞こえにくくなることがあります。

1. ste<u>p</u> / hear<u>t</u> / coo<u>k</u> / Bo<u>b</u> / goo<u>d</u> / big
2. at firs<u>t</u> / in fac<u>t</u>
3. Let's sto<u>p</u>. / Don't drin<u>k</u>. / What a cute ca<u>t</u>! / That's our dog.

Exercise 1 Listen to the CD and choose the statement that best describes the picture.

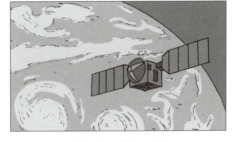

1. (a)   (b)   (c)   2. (a)   (b)   (c)

Exercise 2 Listen to the CD and choose the best response.

1. (a)   (b)   (c)   2. (a)   (b)   (c)   3. (a)   (b)   (c)

Exercise 3 Listen to the CD and choose the best answer.

1. How fast is light?

    (a) Seven times slower than sound

    (b) As fast as the Earth travels around the sun

    (c) Much faster than sound

2. How long does it take the light of the nearest star to reach the Earth?

    (a) More than four years

    (b) About eight minutes

    (c) Not mentioned

Unit 8

● Reading Section ●

Search for Life on Other Planets

Words & Phrases — 次の語句の意味を選びなさい。

1. assume (　)　2. evidence (　)　3. planet (　)　4. fascinating (　)
5. atmosphere (　)　6. moderate (　)　7. galaxy (　)　8. estimate (　)
9. much the same (　)　10. hence (　)

(a) 銀河　　(b) 大気　　(c) 思い込む　　(d) 適度の　　(e) 惑星
(f) 魅惑的な　(g) それゆえ　(h) 推測　　(i) ほぼ同じ　(j) 証拠

次の文を読んで、後の設問に答えなさい。

Reading Passage

　Do you believe in aliens? Or do you think that human beings are the only intelligent life in the universe? Some say that they have received interesting signals from outer space. **Others insist that they have actually seen a UFO.** Still others assume even without any evidence that there must be other intelligent
5　beings somewhere.

　Why do people like to think that there might be life with intelligence on other planets? Indeed, it would be fascinating to believe so, but is that the only reason?

　Let's discuss first what is necessary for life to develop. Atmosphere, water, and moderate temperature are all required. If these are the ideal conditions for a
10　planet to have life, is our Earth the only planet in the whole universe to meet these requirements? Is our home so special?

　The answer is no. Why? Well, have you ever wondered how many sun-like stars there are in our galaxy? According to one estimate, there are at least 100 billion. Besides, our galaxy is not the only galaxy. There are around 100 billion to
15　200 billion galaxies in the universe. If each should have much the same number of stars, how many stars are there in the universe?

　Hence, it's a simple matter of numbers. Maybe one of those billions of stars has a planet with the ideal conditions, like our Earth, on which intelligent life may have developed. So it's quite probable that aliens do exist. If one of those aliens
20　should send a signal to the Earth, would we signal back to them?

(258 words)

intelligent life 知的生命体　　outer space 外宇宙　　meet these requirements この条件を満たす

Science

Exercise 1 （　）内に入る最も適切な語句を選び、文を完成させなさい。

1. The main idea of this passage is that it is (　) that aliens exist.
   (a) certain   (b) likely   (c) unlikely
2. In order for life to develop on a planet, (　) would be necessary.
   (a) soil and moderate temperature   (b) soil and minerals   (c) water and air
3. (　) are said to exist in the universe.
   (a) Thousands of stars   (b) 200 million galaxies   (c) More than 100 billion stars

Exercise 2 次の各文が本文の内容に合っていれば T(True)、合っていなければ F(False) と書きなさい。

____ 1. People like to believe in aliens only because the idea is interesting.

____ 2. The Earth is said to be the only planet that could have life in the universe.

____ 3. Because the universe is huge, there must be some planets with ideal conditions for life somewhere else outside of our Earth.

● Speaking Section ●

「激励」の表現

Exercise 1 強く発音するところの○を黒く塗り、CD を聴いて確認しなさい。次に、英語を見ながら CD を聴いてリピートしなさい。最後に、シャドーイングしなさい。 🎧49

1. A: Oh, no. I flunked the math course. What should I do?

   B: Never mind. It's no big deal. **Better luck next time**!

2. A: My boyfriend left me. He is my third ex in a year. I can't believe it.

   B: You'll soon find another. **Come on, cheer up**!

Exercise 2 次の日本語を見ながら、シャドーイングしなさい。

1. A: あーあ // 落としちゃった / 数学 // どうしよう //

   B: 気にするなよ // たいしたことない // 次に頑張れば //

2. A: 彼に振られちゃった // これで3人目の元彼 / 1年で // 信じられない //

   B: またすぐ見つかるよ / 別の彼が // ほら / 元気出して //

Exercise 3 上記の日本語を見ながら、ペアで交互に英語で会話しなさい。

Unit 8

● Grammar Section ●
形容詞・副詞

★ Grammar Points は Appendix (p.68) を参照

Exercise 1 （　）に入る適切な語句を選びなさい。

1. Tim has been interested in studying biology (late / lately).
2. Every (living / alive) thing on the Earth needs water and air in order to survive.
3. Many researchers at NASA enjoy (expensive / high) salaries.

Exercise 2 2文がほぼ同じ意味になるように、（　）内に入る適切な語を書き入れなさい。

1. No rocket can travel faster than light.
   = It is (　　　) for any rocket to travel faster than light.
2. It was fortunate that he passed the math test. = (　　　), he passed the math test.
3. Many girls but few boys took the computer course.
   = Those who took the computer course were (　　　) girls.

● Writing Section ●
「科学」に関わる表現

Exercise 1 （　）内の語を並べかえて文を完成させなさい。

1. At that time, (Einstein's / scarcely / theory / understood / people) of relativity.
   At that time, _____ of relativity.
2. All the (the / scientists / at / conference / present) were surprised at the discovery.
   All the _____ were surprised at the discovery.

Exercise 2 日本文に合うように適当な英語を補って文を完成させなさい。

1. その惑星と我々の地球は非常に良く似ています。
   The planet and our Earth (　　) (　　) (　　) (　　).
2. 私は未だにニュートンの万有引力の法則が理解できません。
   I (　　) (　　) (　　) Newton's law of universal gravitation.

Exercise 3 日本文を英語に直しなさい。

実際に UFO を見たと主張する人もいます。

_____

Unit 9 Business

● Listening Section ●

Listening Tips

消える音2 — top player はどう聞こえる？—

[p] [t] [k] [b] [d] [g] などの音が単語末に現れ、次に続く単語が子音で始まるときは、最初の単語末が聞こえにくくなることがあり、次の音を発するまで「間」が生じるように聞こえることがあります。

1. top player / part time / black coffee / job behavior / good day / big guy
2. pop song / white dress / sick boy / job hunting / bad movie / big jump

Exercise 1 Listen to the CD and choose the statement that best describes the picture.

1. (a)　(b)　(c)　　　　　　2. (a)　(b)　(c)

Exercise 2 Listen to the CD and choose the best response.

1. (a)　(b)　(c)　　　2. (a)　(b)　(c)　　　3. (a)　(b)　(c)

Exercise 3 Listen to the CD and choose the best answer.

1. Why was the new overpass built in front of Osaka Station?

    (a) Because the number of traffic accidents increased

    (b) Because it was the road to success

    (c) Because the biggest overpass was needed in Japan

2. When did the company build the overpass?

    (a) In the 1960s

    (b) Since 1964

    (c) In 1916

Unit 9

● Reading Section ●

Financial Support of the People's Bank

Words & Phrases 次の語句の意味を選びなさい。

1. repay (　)　　2. manager (　)　　3. loan (　)　　4. provide (　)
5. spread (　)　　6. poverty (　)　　7. improve (　)　　8. dependent (　)
9. appoint (　)　　10. raise (　)

(a) 経営者　(b) 返済する　(c) 貧困　(d) 提供する　(e) 改善する　(f)（日時を）指定する
(g)（問題を）提起する　(h) 依存した　(i) 広まる　(j) 融資する

次の文を読んで、後の設問に答えなさい。

Reading Passage

　How can you lend money to poor people who may not repay, if you are a bank manager? The economist Muhammad Yunus, who set up a bank for the poor people in Bangladesh in 1983, began to loan small amounts of money to the poor to solve this problem.

5　The system of providing small loans started locally, but it continued to spread and became bigger and bigger. This system has been applied in many countries, including the U.S., the U.K., France, and Japan. They are developed countries, but surprisingly, there is a lot of poverty there.

　The Yunus system is as follows. First, five unrelated people with the same
10 goal get together to improve their lives. Since the members are not related to one another, they can build good relationships without being dependent on each other. The members then have to take an interview. After passing this interview, two of them receive the money. **If the first two pay the money back by the appointed time, the next three receive a loan next.**

15　By supporting the economic independence of the poor, Yunus was awarded the Nobel Peace Prize in 2006. Like ODA, this loan service is not a charity project that gives money, builds a school, or digs a well. He has made a system that helps poor people have more opportunities to be independent. His endeavor is not only for helping the poor, but also raising an issue in society.

(238 words)

Muhammad Yunus バングラデシュの経済学者・グラミン銀行の創設者で、そこを起源とする少額融資（マイクロクレジット）の創始者　unrelated people 血縁でない人々　related 血縁の　pay back（借金など）を返す　independence 自立　ODA (official development assistance) 政府開発援助

Business

Exercise 1 （　）内に入る最も適切な語句を選び、文を完成させなさい。

1. The passage is mainly about how a bank can help the poor become economically (　　).
   (a) independent　　(b) dependent　　(c) wasteful
2. The bank not only gives money, but also helps the poor (　　).
   (a) clean a well　　(b) have opportunities to be more independent　　(c) beg for food
3. (　　) countries in the world have a system of providing small loans now.
   (a) Every　　(b) None of　　(c) Not all

Exercise 2 次の各文が本文の内容に合っていれば T(True)、合っていなければ F(False) と書きなさい。

_____　1. Financial support for the poor is no longer needed in developed countries.
_____　2. In order to borrow money, people form a group with their families.
_____　3. When someone in the group does not repay by the due date in the first place, the bank does not lend money to the other members.

● Speaking Section ●
「賛同」の表現

Exercise 1 強く発音するところの○を黒く塗り、CD を聴いて確認しなさい。次に、英語を見ながら CD を聴いてリピートしなさい。最後に、シャドーイングしなさい。

1. A: We are going to see a play tonight. Do you want to join us?

   B: Yeah! **I'd love to**. I haven't watched plays for ages.

2. A: The play has finished. I think the theme of the play was difficult to understand.

   B: **I agree with** you. It was a waste of time.

Exercise 2 次の日本語を見ながら、シャドーイングしなさい。

1. A: 出かけるんだよ / 観劇に / 今夜 // 一緒に行く //

   B: はい // ぜひ // 劇など観たことがないわ / 長い間 //

2. A: 劇は終わったね // 思う / 劇の主題が / 分かりにくかった //

   B: その通り // 時間の無駄だったね //

Exercise 3 上記の日本語を見ながら、ペアで交互に英語で会話しなさい。

Unit 9

● **Grammar Section** ●

前置詞

★ Grammar Points は Appendix (p.69) を参照

Exercise 1 （ ）に入る適切な語句を選びなさい。

1. My boss should arrive here (until / by) 4 p.m.
2. The section chief took the Shinkansen train (from / till) Osaka to Tokyo.
3. I did not like working (at / in) that dark blue uniform.

Exercise 2 2文がほぼ同じ意味になるように、（ ）内に入る適切な語を書き入れなさい。

1. I worked here as an Italian chef before.
   = I worked here as an Italian chef (   ) the past.
2. I got the position offer information via the Internet.
   = I got the position offer information (   ) way of the Internet.
3. I considered the offer of the merger carefully. After that I accepted it.
   = (   ) careful consideration, I accepted the offer of the merger.

● **Writing Section** ●

「ビジネス」に関わる表現

Exercise 1 （ ）内の語を並べかえて文を完成させなさい。

1. Which (do / in / you / work / department)?
   Which _____?
2. I will attend the (behalf / on / of / my / meeting) colleague.
   I will attend the _____ colleague.

Exercise 2 日本文に合うように適当な英語を補って文を完成させなさい。

1. そのプロジェクトは先週、台風のため中止されました。
   The project was canceled because (   ) (   ) (   ) last week.
2. 母の仕事は、貧しい人々を助けることに関するものです。
   My mother's job is something concerned (   ) (   ) (   ) poor.

Exercise 3 日本文を英語に直しなさい。

期日までに、そのローンを返済できますか。

_____

Unit 10 Social Issues

● Listening Section ●

Listening Tips

消える音３ — **call him** はどう聞こえる？—

くだけた会話や速いスピードの発話では、強勢の置かれない音節で次のような現象の起こることがあります。

1. 曖昧母音 [ə] の消失　　ca<u>me</u>ra / sev<u>e</u>ral / fav<u>o</u>rite

2. [h] や [ð] の脱落　　I call <u>him</u>.　/ I'll send <u>them</u>.

Exercise 1 *Listen to the CD and choose the statement that best describes the picture.*

1. (a)　(b)　(c)　　　　　2. (a)　(b)　(c)

Exercise 2 *Listen to the CD and choose the best response.*

1. (a)　(b)　(c)　　　　2. (a)　(b)　(c)　　　　3. (a)　(b)　(c)

Exercise 3 *Listen to the CD and choose the best answer.*

1. Which of the following is a great inconvenience in a crowded space?

    (a) Talking loudly

    (b) Looking at smartphones while walking

    (c) Playing football

2. Which is NOT mentioned as a reason for people using their smartphones while walking?

    (a) Making a phone call

    (b) Sending a message

    (c) Playing a game

Unit 10

● Reading Section ●

Passive Smoking

Words & Phrases 次の語句の意味を選びなさい。

1. separate (　)　2. ban (　)　3. restrict (　)　4. public transportation (　)
5. norm (　)　6. fuss (　)　7. the former (　)　8. the latter (　)
9. concentration (　)　10. harmful chemicals (　)

　　(a) 標準　　(b) 前者　　(c) 規制する　　(d) 分離する　　(e) 有害化学物質
　　(f) 後者　　(g) 濃度　　(h) 禁止する　　(i) 大騒ぎ　　(j) 公共交通機関

次の文を読んで、後の設問に答えなさい。

Reading Passage

　Passive smoking means that you take in tobacco smoke even if you are not a smoker. Today, in many restaurants and coffee shops, smoking and non-smoking areas are separated. Also, in most universities, smoking on campus is banned or severely restricted. In addition, public transportation is mostly smoke-free, and
5 non-smoking flights are the norm.
　Moreover, lots of announcements are made and warning signs put up to keep people from smoking in public spaces. Smokers might wonder what all the fuss is about. Is secondhand smoke (SHS) so bad? Why is passive smoking a problem?
　There are two kinds of SHS: mainstream smoke and sidestream smoke. The
10 former is the smoke exhaled by a smoker. The latter is from the end of a lit cigarette, which has higher concentrations of chemicals that can cause cancer. This is more toxic than mainstream smoke. When non-smokers breathe in SHS, they take in nicotine and other harmful chemicals the same way smokers do. As you breathe in more SHS, there will be more of these toxic substances in your body.
15 　SHS is known to have at least 70 harmful chemicals that can cause cancer. If smokers die because of their bad habits, that's their problem. However, if non-smokers die because of SHS, it's a social problem. In earlier days, when smoking was not so severely restricted, restaurants and cafes did not separate smokers from non-smokers. **Even today, people are free to smoke in many pubs and bars**
20 **in Japan**. We still have a long way to go.

(255 words)

mainstream smoke 主流煙　　sidestream smoke 副流煙　　exhale 吐き出す　　toxic 有毒な

46

Social Issues

Exercise 1 （　）内に入る最も適切な語句を選び、文を完成させなさい。

1. This passage is mainly about (　) caused by tobacco smoke.
   (a) diseases　　(b) benefits　　(c) problems
2. Non-smoking signs can often be found in (　).
   (a) coffee shops　　(b) public spaces　　(c) private houses
3. Mainstream smoke is (　) sidestream smoke.
   (a) less toxic than　　(b) more toxic than　　(c) as toxic as

Exercise 2 次の各文が本文の内容に合っていれば T(True)、合っていなければ F(False) と書きなさい。

____ 1. Today, quite a few restaurants have a separated non-smoking area.

____ 2. Only the smoke exhaled by a smoker is called SHS.

____ 3. It won't be long before we realize a smoke-free society.

● Speaking Section ●

「反対」の表現

Exercise 1 強く発音するところの○を黒く塗り、CD を聴いて確認しなさい。次に、英語を見ながら CD を聴いてリピートしなさい。最後に、シャドーイングしなさい。

1. A: I'm quite sure Cindy is coming to our seniors' farewell party.

   B: **Well, I doubt it**. She said she'd be very busy this week writing a paper.

2. A: A typhoon is coming. It'll hit Osaka. Then, all the classes will be canceled.

   B: **I'm afraid not**. A typhoon often changes its course. You can't expect it too much.

Exercise 2 次の日本語を見ながら、シャドーイングしなさい。

1. A: きっと / シンディは来てくれるよね / 先輩たちの / 送別会に //
   B: さあそれはどうかな // 彼女言ってたよ / とても忙しいって / 今週 / レポートを書くのに //
2. A: 台風が来てるよ // 大阪を直撃するよ // そうしたら / 全ての授業が / 休講だね //
   B: だめだろうね // 台風はよく / コースを変えるからね // 期待しすぎちゃだめだよ //

Exercise 3 上記の日本語を見ながら、ペアで交互に英語で会話しなさい。

Unit 10

● **Grammar Section** ●
接続詞

★ Grammar Points は Appendix (p.69) を参照

Exercise 1 （ ）に入る適切な語句を選びなさい。

1. I watched a documentary titled "Let's Quit Smoking" last night, (and / but) it was a lot of fun.
2. Puerto Ricans suffered a lot (that / when) a big hurricane hit them.
3. (Since / While) smoking is permitted in some bars, trains are mostly smoke-free.

Exercise 2 2文がほぼ同じ意味になるように、（ ）内に入る適切な語を書き入れなさい。

1. The Internet is convenient, but there's a lot of danger in it.
   = Even (   ) the Internet is convenient, there's a lot of danger in it.
2. The low birth rate will make it important to depend on a foreign workforce.
   = There are fewer and fewer children in Japan, (   ) it is important to depend on workers from abroad.
3. Turn the tap all the way off, and you can save more water.
   = (   ) you turn the tap all the way off, more water will be saved.

● **Writing Section** ●
「社会問題」に関わる表現

Exercise 1 （ ）内の語を並べかえて文を完成させなさい。

1. We must seriously (we / make / discuss / whether / should) more use of nuclear power.
   We must seriously _____ more use of nuclear power.
2. Young children must not use smart phones freely, (lot / are / since / a / there) of bad Web sites.
   Young children must not use smart phones freely, _____ of bad Web-sites.

Exercise 2 日本文に合うように適当な英語を補って文を完成させなさい。

1. 列車内では、他の乗客の迷惑にならないよう、スマートフォンのボリュームを下げなさい。（while を用いて）
   Turn down the volume on your smartphone (   ) (   ) (   ) on the train so as not to bother other passengers.
2. 女性の多くは、仮に常勤の仕事に就いていても、家事の助けを何ら受けていません。
   Many women, even (   ) (   ) (   ) full-time, get no help with housework.

Exercise 3 日本文を英語に直しなさい。

あなたの国では、パブやバーで自由にタバコを吸えますか。

_____

Unit 11 Natural Disasters

● **Listening Section** ●

Listening Tips

つながる音 1 — kick off はどう聞こえる？—

子音で終わる語の直後に母音で始まる語が続くと、子音と母音の連結が起こり、1つの語のように聞こえることがあります。

1. kick off   2. check in   3. laugh at   4. give in
5. an orange   6. Come on!   7. watch out   8. depend on

Exercise 1 Listen to the CD and choose the statement that best describes the picture.

1. (a)　(b)　(c)　　　　　2. (a)　(b)　(c)

Exercise 2 Listen to the CD and choose the best response.

1. (a)　(b)　(c)　　　2. (a)　(b)　(c)　　　3. (a)　(b)　(c)

Exercise 3 Listen to the CD and choose the best answer.

1. What should we do in a house during an earthquake?

    (a) Go outside of the house.

    (b) Turn off the gas.

    (c) Depend on any information you get.

2. Which is important during an earthquake?

    (a) To gather correct information

    (b) To call family members

    (c) To depend on one source of information

Unit 11

● **Reading Section** ●

Hope for the Best and Prepare for the Worst.

Words & Phrases 次の語句の意味を選びなさい。

1. disaster ( )   2. earthquake ( )   3. volcanic ( )   4. eruption ( )
5. typhoon ( )   6. torrential ( )   7. unprecedented ( )   8. victim ( )
9. evacuation ( )   10. drill ( )

(a) 地震   (b) 犠牲者   (c) 噴火   (d) 避難   (e) 災害
(f) 未曽有の   (g) 土砂降りの   (h) 火山の   (i) 訓練   (j) 台風

次の文を読んで、後の設問に答えなさい。

Reading Passage

　Japan is a country prone to natural disasters, such as earthquakes, tsunamis, volcanic eruptions, floods, and typhoons. Recent earthquakes include the Osaka Earthquake in 2018, the Kumamoto Earthquake in 2016, the Great East Japan Earthquake in 2011, which triggered a massive tsunami, and the Great Hanshin-Awaji Earthquake in 1995. As for volcanic eruptions, *Kusatsu Shirane-san* and *Shinmoedake* erupted in 2018, *Ontake-san* in 2014, and *Unzen-fugen-dake* in 1991. Moreover, abnormal weather phenomena such as typhoons and torrential rainfall are happening more frequently recently. These are said to be associated with the effects of global warming.

　These disasters and severe weather events are often described as "unprecedented" or the "worst in decades." They have killed or injured thousands and affected economic development and social life in Japan. We have to act promptly to protect ourselves against such unprecedented disasters.

　The Japanese government and local governments should take adequate actions, such as making antidisaster plans and issuing evacuation orders. Disaster drills for local residents are also important to see if the evacuation plans really work.

　However, we should not depend on the government alone, but should create a family disaster plan by ourselves. First, we should know what disasters are possible in our area, and then talk with our family about how to prepare and respond if a disaster happens. For example, we should know about what to do if our family members are not together. Being familiar with escape routes is also essential. Discussing disasters ahead of time will help reduce fear and anxiety. Hope for the best and prepare for the worst.

(261 words)

prone to ～ ～しやすい　　abnormal weather phenomenon 異常気象現象　　worst in decades 数十年で最悪の
antidisaster plan 防災計画　　evacuation 避難　　Hope for the best and prepare for the worst. 備えあれば憂いなし

Disaster

Exercise 1 （ ）内に入る最も適切な語句を選び、文を完成させなさい。

1. This passage focuses mainly on (   ).

    (a) volcanic eruptions　　(b) natural disasters　　(c) global warming

2. Japan has experienced (   ) volcanic eruptions since 1991.

    (a) at most two　　(b) at most three　　(c) at least four

3. We (   ) depend only on the government to prepare for disasters.

    (a) can　　(b) must not　　(c) will

Exercise 2 次の各文が本文の内容に合っていれば T(True)、合っていなければ F(False) と書きなさい。

_____ 1. A tsunami occurred after the Great Hanshin-Awaji Earthquake.

_____ 2. Natural disasters have taken many lives, but have not affected the economy in Japan.

_____ 3. We should be familiar with disasters that may occur in our areas.

● Speaking Section ●

「承諾」の表現

Exercise 1 強く発音するところの○を黒く塗り、CD を聴いて確認しなさい。次に、英語を見ながら CD を聴いてリピートしなさい。最後に、シャドーイングしなさい。

1. A: Will you show me how to use my smartphone?
      ○ ○ ○ ○ ○○ ○○   ○   ○

   B: **Sure**. It's not so difficult. You can do many things with your smartphone.
      ○   ○ ○   ○○   ○ ○ ○   ○   ○   ○   ○   ○

2. A: Can you wait here for a minute?
      ○   ○   ○   ○   ○   ○○

   B: **No problem.** Please take your time to look around the shop.
      ○   ○   ○   ○   ○   ○   ○   ○○   ○   ○

Exercise 2 次の日本語を見ながら、シャドーイングしなさい。

1. A: 教えてもらえる / 使い方を / 私のスマートフォンの //

   B: もちろん // そんなに難しくないよ // 色々できるよ / あなたのスマートフォンで //

2. A: ここで待ってもらえる / ちょっと //

   B: いいよ // どうぞゆっくりして / 店を見て回って //

Exercise 3 上記の日本語を見ながら、ペアで交互に英語で会話しなさい。

Unit 11

● Grammar Section ●
比較

★ Grammar Points は Appendix (p.70) を参照

Exercise 1 （ ）に入る適切な語句を選びなさい。

1. Which is (more dangerous / most dangerous), an earthquake or a typhoon?
2. Which typhoon was (the biggest / bigger) in this century in Japan?
3. Typhoons are happening (frequently / more frequently) than volcanic eruptions.

Exercise 2 （ ）内に入る適切な語を書き入れなさい。

1. Earthquakes are the (   ) terrible of all natural disasters.
2. These disasters and severe weather events are (   ) worst in decades.
3. Disaster drills for local residents are more important (   ) any other drill.

● Writing Section ●
「災害」に関わる表現

Exercise 1 （ ）内の語を並べかえて文を完成させなさい。

1. (in / more / occur / frequently / earthquakes) Japan than in other countries.
   _____ Japan than in other countries.

2. This volcanic (is / eruption / in / largest / the) this century.
   This volcanic _____ this century.

Exercise 2 日本文に合うように適当な英語を補って文を完成させなさい。

1. 東日本大震災は、阪神・淡路大震災よりも多くの人の命を奪いました。
   The Great East Japan Earthquake killed (   ) (   ) (   ) the Great Hanshin-Awaji Earthquake.

2. この台風は前の台風よりもかなり大きい。
   This typhoon (   ) (   ) (   ) (   ) the last one.

Exercise 3 日本文を英語に直しなさい。

日本政府は今回は適切な行動を取りました。

_____

Unit 12 International Issues

● Listening Section ●

---**Listening Tips**---

つながる音２ — next year はどう聞こえる？—

子音で終わる語の直後に子音 [j] で始まる語が続くと、子音と [j] が相互に影響し合い、全く別の音のように聞こえることがあります。

1. next year / meet you　　　[t] + [j] ➡ [tʃ]　　2. did you / would you　　[d] + [j] ➡ [dʒ]
3. miss you / God bless you!　[s] + [j] ➡ [ʃ]　　4. as usual / as you know　[z] + [j] ➡ [ʒ]

Exercise 1 Listen to the CD and choose the statement that best describes the picture.

　　1. (a)　(b)　(c)　　　　　　　　2. (a)　(b)　(c)

Exercise 2 Listen to the CD and choose the best response.

1. (a)　(b)　(c)　　　2. (a)　(b)　(c)　　　3. (a)　(b)　(c)

Exercise 3 Listen to the CD and choose the best answer.

1. When did international aid start?
    (a) After World War II
    (b) After developing countries were discussed in the news
    (c) After we found a solution to the difficult problem in society

2. What is NOT mentioned as a problem which developing countries have?
    (a) Water
    (b) Agriculture
    (c) Energy

Unit 12

● Reading Section ●

Fairtrade Products

Words & Phrases 次の語句の意味を選びなさい。

1. crop (　)　　2. region (　)　　3. currency (　)　　4. purchase (　)
5. present (　)　6. sufficient (　)　7. reduce (　)　　8. guarantee (　)
9. appropriate (　)　10. description (　)

(a) 農作物　　(b) 通貨　　(c) 十分な　　(d) 適正な　　(e) 記載
(f) 減らす　　(g) 現在　　(h) 購入　　(i) 地域　　(j) 保証する

次の文を読んで、後の設問に答えなさい。

Reading Passage

　We have Valentine's Day in February. Do you usually eat chocolates on Valentine's Day? **If so, have you ever thought about how chocolate is made?**

　Chocolate is made from cacao. Cacao is a crop grown in tropical regions. In the past, it was also used as currency. However, the purchase price of cacao is very low at present. Due to this reason, farmers cannot employ sufficient workers. As a result, children are made to work from morning till evening, so they cannot go to school.

　Various efforts are being made in order to reduce child labor or to improve the situation of workers and farmers as much as possible. One of them is Fairtrade. Fairtrade is a movement that involves buying and selling things. It guarantees that the people who produce goods receive an appropriate price for them. We can help workers earn fair wages by buying Fairtrade products, even though they are a little more expensive.

　To check whether a product is a Fairtrade product, look at the package. The description will say "This product is Fairtrade," or you will see the FAIRTRADE label on it. When you buy Fairtrade goods as consumers, you are making your opinions known to society. Why don't you all try to buy a Fairtrade product once? It is a good way to reduce poverty and to feel happy by doing so. Fairtrade products are not limited to chocolate. There are also Fairtrade coffee, tea, fruits, flowers, and so on. Try looking for other Fairtrade products besides them. Your choices may change the world.

(260 words)

cacao 熱帯地域で育つ農作物（昔は高価で通貨としても使われていたが、現在ではカカオの買い取り価格は安く、店頭でチョコレートを購入した時に支払う金額のうち生産者の収入となるのはごく僅か）　due to ～ ～のために　improve 改善する　Fairtrade 公正取引き（発展途上国で作られた農作物や製品を適正な価格で取引きすることによって、生産者の生活向上を支える仕組み）　earn wages 賃金を得る　consumer 消費者

International Issues

Exercise 1 （　）内に入る最も適切な語句を選び、文を完成させなさい。

1. This passage focuses mainly on the (　) of Fairtrade.
   (a) aim   (b) products   (c) prosperity
2. The Fairtrade system (　) that the people who produce goods get a fair price.
   (a) makes sense   (b) makes certain   (c) makes good
3. The Fairtrade system offers a chance for (　) to assist people living in poverty.
   (a) producers   (b) children   (c) consumers

Exercise 2 次の各文が本文の内容に合っていれば T(True)、合っていなければ F(False) と書きなさい。

_____ 1. Children are used in the workforce in some countries now.
_____ 2. In the Fairtrade system, we can buy quality products at a low price.
_____ 3. If you purchase Fairtrade products, it can help producers improve their quality of life.

● Speaking Section ●

「忠告」の表現

Exercise 1 強く発音するところの○を黒く塗り、CD を聴いて確認しなさい。次に、英語を見ながら CD を聴いてリピートしなさい。最後に、シャドーイングしなさい。

1. A: My head and stomach hurt. I may have a fever.
   ○ ○ ○　○　　○　○ ○ ○ ○

   B: You look pale. **You had better** see the doctor.
   ○ ○ ○　○ ○ ○　　　○ ○ ○

2. A: How can I get to the station? Is it a long way from this hotel?
   ○ ○ ○ ○ ○ ○　○ ○ ○ ○　○　○　○

   B: There is a shuttle bus which leaves the hotel every twenty minutes.
   ○ ○ ○ ○ ○ ○ ○　○ ○ ○　○　○

   You should take the bus.
   ○　　○　　○　○ ○

Exercise 2 次の日本語を見ながら、シャドーイングしなさい。

1. A: 頭もお腹も / 痛い // 熱もあるみたい //
   B: 顔色が悪いね // 診てもらった方がいいよ / お医者さんに //
2. A: どうしたら / 駅に行けますか // 遠いですか / このホテルから //
   B: シャトルバスがあります / ホテルから出ています / 20分ごとに // 乗れば良いです / そのバスに //

Exercise 3 上記の日本語を見ながら、ペアで交互に英語で会話しなさい。

Unit 12

● Grammar Section ●
関係代名詞

★ Grammar Points は Appendix (p.70) を参照

Exercise 1 （ ）に入る適切な語句を選びなさい。

1. The foreign ship, (whose / which) left the port, was greatly damaged.
2. This is the tourist information office (at which / which) I visited last week.
3. Malala was the student (who / what) won the Nobel Peace Prize in Pakistan.

Exercise 2 （ ）内に入る適切な語を書き入れなさい。

1. I have an aunt. She emigrated from Europe.
   = I have an aunt (   ) emigrated from Europe.
2. I know a boy. His father is a diplomat.
   = I know a boy (   ) father is a diplomat.
3. He said the suit was made in Italy. That was a lie.
   = He said the suit was made in Italy, (   ) was a lie.

● Writing Section ●
「国際問題」に関わる表現

Exercise 1 （ ）内の語を並べかえて文を完成させなさい。

1. WHO identified the (which / virus / the / caused / flu) in Northeast Asia.
   WHO identified the _____ in Northeast Asia.
2. I know the foreign exchange (were / you / to / talking / student) at the party.
   I know the foreign exchange _____ at the party.

Exercise 2 日本文に合うように適当な英語を補って文を完成させなさい。

1. アフリカは、もはや昔のアフリカではありません。
   Africa is (   ) (   ) (   ) used to be any more.
2. 私は、住んでみたい国がたくさんあります。
   There are many countries (   ) (   ) (   ) want to live.

Exercise 3 日本文を英語に直しなさい。

あなたはこれまで、チョコレートが何から作られているのかを考えたことがありますか。

_____

Unit 13 Technology

● Listening Section ●

Listening Tips

アメリカ英語の発音 — **letter** はどう聞こえる？—

アメリカ英語の発音の特徴として、特にカジュアルな会話や速い発話の場合、以下の特徴が見られることがあります。

1. 母音と母音に挟まれた [t] が日本語のラ行音に近い音に変化　　le<u>tt</u>er / cu<u>t</u> out
2. [n] に [t] が続く場合、[n] が後続する [t] に影響され、[n] に変わる傾向
   ce<u>nt</u>er / i<u>nt</u>ernational / the I<u>nt</u>ernet
3. 短縮表現　　I'm <u>going to</u> eat out. → I'm <u>gonna</u> eat out.
   I <u>want to</u> go swimming. → I <u>wanna</u> go swimming.

Exercise 1 Listen to the CD and choose the statement that best describes the picture.

1. (a)　(b)　(c)　　　　　　　　2. (a)　(b)　(c)

Exercise 2 Listen to the CD and choose the best response.

1. (a)　(b)　(c)　　　2. (a)　(b)　(c)　　　3. (a)　(b)　(c)

Exercise 3 Listen to the CD and choose the best answer.

1. When will the event be held?
   (a) March 13
   (b) March 20
   (c) March 30

2. What will be seen at the exposition?
   (a) Video projectors for home use
   (b) Goods sold at convenience stores
   (c) Home devices connected to the Internet

Unit 13

● **Reading Section** ●

Hopes and Concerns about Robot Technology

Words & Phrases 次の語句の意味を選びなさい。

1. automated ( ) 2. perform ( ) 3. human ( ) 4. demanding ( )
5. humanoid ( ) 6. revolutionize ( ) 7. improve ( ) 8. emotion ( )
9. deal with ( ) 10. relationship ( )

(a) 人間　　(b) 遂行する　(c) 対処する　(d) 上達させる　(e) 革命を起こす
(f) 人型ロボット　(g) きつい　(h) 関係　(i) 感情　(j) 自動化された

次の文を読んで、後の設問に答えなさい。

Reading Passage

　Robots, robots, robots. AI-powered robots are around us everywhere, at home, at work, and at factories. **Whether we are aware of it or not, robots are finding their way into our lives.** An automated robot vacuum cleaner sweeps floors clean at home, industrial robots are in operation at factories, nursing-care robots take care of the elderly, and robot arms help doctors with operations. Robots can perform jobs that are difficult or impossible for humans to do. In the not-too-distant future, we will be leaving it to robots to do most of the "3D" jobs — Demanding, Dirty, and Dangerous.

　How about the service industry? Humanoids welcome guests and customers with a smile and interact with them at hotels, stores, and event sites. For example, robots give customers directions and answer various questions. Robots are also expected to revolutionize education. For example, English-speaking robots can help learners improve English conversation skills.

　Impressed? Certainly, technology has made our lives easier, more convenient, and more comfortable than ever before. But does it truly make us happier? We are worried that we may lose our jobs to robots. These jobs include the ones that require highly-skilled mental work and intelligence.

　What we fear most is that robots may have humanlike emotion. Rather, such robots may have already been developed. We are concerned that human uniqueness may be lost and we may be under the control of the robots we have developed. How should we deal with robots? What will the human-robot relationship be like? There are many unanswered questions ahead of us.

(257 words)

AI = artificial intelligence 人工知能　　robot vacuum cleaner お掃除ロボット　　nursing-care robots 介護ロボット　　leave ～ to robots ～をロボットに任せる　　interact with 交流する　　highly-skilled 高度な技術の　　be under the control of the robots ロボットにコントロールされる

Technology

Exercise 1 （ ）内に入る最も適切な語句を選び、文を完成させなさい。

1. This passage focuses mainly on the (　) of AI-based robots.
   (a) convenience　　　(b) problems　　　(c) for and against opinions
2. In English education, robots are used to improve learners' (　) ability.
   (a) reading　　　(b) speaking　　　(c) writing
3. The author fears most that robots may have humanlike (　).
   (a) looks　　　(b) intelligence　　　(c) feelings

Exercise 2 次の各文が本文の内容に合っていれば T(True)、合っていなければ F(False) と書きなさい。

____ 1. In the future, robots will do most dangerous jobs hand in hand with humans.

____ 2. Robots have already replaced human workers at the workplace completely.

____ 3. The author questions whether or not high-tech robots make us happier.

● Speaking Section ●

「感想」の表現

Exercise 1 強く発音するところの○を黒く塗り、CD を聴いて確認しなさい。次に、英語を見ながら CD を聴いてリピートしなさい。最後に、シャドーイングしなさい。

1. A: You visited the World Heritage Site, didn't you? How did you feel about it?

   B: It was great. **It is the most memorable experience I've ever had**.

2. A: What do you think of Harry's performance? I was deeply moved.

   B: **Very disappointing, I should say. That was not as good as I expected**.

Exercise 2 次の日本語を見ながら、シャドーイングしなさい。

1. A: 訪ねたんだよね / その世界遺産に // どう思った //

   B: すごかったよ // それは / 最も記憶に残る経験だったよ / 今までの中で //

2. A: どう思う / ハリーの演技 // 私はとても感動したよ //

   B: とてもがっかり / ってとこかな // 良くなかった / 思った程には //

Exercise 3 上記の日本語を見ながら、ペアで交互に英語で会話しなさい。

Unit 13

● **Grammar Section** ●
関係副詞

★ Grammar Points は Appendix (p.71) を参照

Exercise 1 （ ）に入る適切な語句を選びなさい。

1. Tell me the reason (how / why) driverless vehicles are needed.
2. I will explain (how / while) the suspension bridge was constructed.
3. This is the plant (when / where) the latest IoT products are manufactured.

Exercise 2 （ ）内に入る適切な語を書き入れなさい。

1. The day may come. On that day, machine translation will replace human translators.
   = The day may come (　　　) machine translation will replace human translators.
2. Cell phones are being replaced by smartphones. Let me explain the reason.
   = Let me explain the reason (　　　) cell phones are being replaced by smartphones.
3. It looks like we've stepped into the area. The GPS doesn't work here.
   = It looks like we've stepped into the area (　　　) the GPS doesn't work.

● **Writing Section** ●
「科学技術」に関わる表現

Exercise 1 （ ）内の語を並べかえて文を完成させなさい。

1. E-learning is one of the promising (education / technology / meets / where / areas).
   E-learning is one of the promising _____.
2. I can't imagine (when / the / will / day / drones) deliver various goods directly to customers' homes from factories.
   I can't imagine _____ deliver various goods directly to customers' homes from factories.

Exercise 2 日本文に合うように適当な英語を補って文を完成させなさい。

1. 今日の最新技術が過去の事物になってしまう日が来るかもしれません。
   The day may come (　　) (　　) (　　) (　　) will become a thing of the past.
2. なぜ私のコンピューターがハッカーに攻撃されたのか理解できません。
   (　　) (　　) (　　) (　　) my computer was attacked by hackers.

Exercise 3 日本文を英語に直しなさい。

好むと好まざるとにかかわらず、コンピューターは我々の生活に入り込んでいます。

Unit 14 Music

● **Listening Section** ●

Listening Tips

イギリス英語の発音 — can't はどう聞こえる？—

アメリカ英語の発音と比較・対照すると、イギリス英語の発音は特に母音に関して以下の特徴が見られます。

例	イギリス英語	アメリカ英語
1. can't / ask	[kɑːnt] / [ɑːsk]	[kænt] / [æsk]
2. hot / shop	[hɔt] / [ʃɔp]	[hat] / [ʃap]
3. car / park	[kɑː] / [pɑːk]	[kɑːr] / [pɑːrk]

Exercise 1 *Listen to the CD and choose the statement that best describes the picture.*

1. (a)   (b)   (c)   2. (a)   (b)   (c)

Exercise 2 *Listen to the CD and choose the best response.*

1. (a)   (b)   (c)   2. (a)   (b)   (c)   3. (a)   (b)   (c)

Exercise 3 *Listen to the CD and choose the best answer.*

1. What is the feature of the festival?

   (a) Russian music

   (b) Hawaiian music

   (c) Ballet music

2. What event will be held on the last day?

   (a) A ballet contest

   (b) A social dance contest

   (c) A singing contest

Unit 14

● **Reading Section** ●

The Power of Music

Words & Phrases — 次の語句の意味を選びなさい。

1. universal ( )   2. united ( )   3. motivating ( )   4. depressed ( )
5. enhance ( )   6. healing ( )   7. console ( )   8. calm down ( )
9. benefit ( )   10. therapy ( )

(a) 慰める   (b) 癒す   (c) やる気を起こす   (d) 団結している   (e) 落ち着く
(f) 治療法   (g) 高める   (h) 普遍的な   (i) 利益を与える   (j) 落ち込んでいる

次の文を読んで、後の設問に答えなさい。

Reading Passage

Have you ever felt the power of music? Why does music attract us so much? Many reasons come to mind.

Music is universal. When people from different countries sing in a chorus or perform in an orchestra, they can communicate with each other through music even if they don't understand their fellow members' languages. Through music, we can make friends with each other and feel united. Music can bring people together.

Music is motivating. When we feel depressed, it is helpful to listen to our favorite music. This is because when a pleasure-related stimulus is given, a feel-good chemical is released in the brain. That is why music can enhance our positive mood.

Music is healing. Music consoles and comforts us. When we feel nervous, music helps us to relax and calm down. When we are under stress, music can reduce our stress and lower our anxiety. The healing power of music can benefit anyone, young or old.

The healing power of music is not only psychological. This is where music therapy comes in. Music therapy explores the effect of music on various diseases. For example, research suggests that listening to music may benefit heart disease patients by controlling heart rate and reducing blood pressure. Music therapy can be receptive, which means that merely listening to music played by therapists can benefit patients.

We sincerely hope **more research will be done to find out the potential of music on various aspects of our health and our lives**.

(247 words)

come to mind 心に浮かぶ   fellow members 仲間   pleasure-related 快楽に関連した   stimulus 刺激   feel-good chemical 快感化学物質（dopamine ドーパミンなど）   psychological 心理的な   explore 探索する   heart rate 心拍数   blood pressure 血圧   receptive 受動的な   therapist 治療士

Music

Exercise 1 （　）内に入る最も適切な語句を選び、文を完成させなさい。

1. The main idea of this passage is why we are (　) the power of music.
   (a) excited by　　　(b) upset by　　　(c) attracted by
2. We feel (　) when we are singing in a chorus.
   (a) healed　　　(b) united　　　(c) motivated
3. If you listen to your favorite music, (　) will be released in the brain.
   (a) a chemical　　　(b) stimulus　　　(c) treatment effects

Exercise 2 次の各文が本文の内容に合っていればT(True)、合っていなければF(False)と書きなさい。

____　1. Music helps to reduce stress and anxiety.

____　2. Music therapy has only good psychological effects.

____　3. In music therapy, patients have to play a musical instrument.

● Speaking Section ●

「別れ」の表現

Exercise 1 強く発音するところの○を黒く塗り、CDを聴いて確認しなさい。次に、英語を見ながらCDを聴いてリピートしなさい。最後に、シャドーイングしなさい。

1. A: **I must be going now. It was good talking with you.**

   B: Oh! **Can't you stay a little longer?** No? Then let me drive you home.

2. A: As soon as I get home, I'll email you.

   B: Please do. **Let's keep in touch. Take care.**

Exercise 2 次の日本語を見ながら、シャドーイングしなさい。

1. A: もう行かなくては // 良かった / 一緒に話せて //
   B: えー // いてもらえない / もう少し // だめ // じゃあ / 車で家まで送るよ //
2. A: 家についたらすぐに / メールを送るね //
   B: そうして // 連絡取り合おうね // 体に気をつけてね //

Exercise 3 上記の日本語を見ながら、ペアで交互に英語で会話しなさい。

Unit 14

● Grammar Section ●
仮定法

★ Grammar Points は Appendix (p.71) を参照

Exercise 1 ( ) に入る適切な語句を選びなさい。

1. Without music, our life (will / would) not be as exciting or interesting.
2. He sings (as / when) if he were a professional opera singer.
3. I (want / wish) I could play the piano well.

Exercise 2 ( ) 内に入る適切な語を書き入れなさい。

1. If he had participated in the contest, he (　　　) have won the first prize.
2. If it (　　　) not for music, figure skating would not be as artistic and impressive.
3. I'm studying at a music school in Japan. I (　　　) I could go to the Juilliard School.

● Writing Section ●
「音楽」に関わる表現

Exercise 1 ( ) 内の語を並べかえて文を完成させなさい。

1. If I had started playing the violin earlier, I (violinist / would / a / concert / be) now.
   If I had started playing the violin earlier, _____ now.
2. (Beethoven / lived / had / if / longer), would he have composed a 10th symphony?
   _____, would he have composed a 10th symphony?

Exercise 2 日本文に合うように適当な英語を補って文を完成させなさい。

1. 多くの人がネットから音楽をダウンロードしなければ、CD の売り上げは激減しないでしょう。
   The sale of (　　) (　　) (　　) (　　) sharply if many people did not download music from the Internet.
2. もし奨学金をもらえていたら、海外で音楽を勉強できたでしょう。
   If I had won the scholarship, I (　　) (　　) (　　) (　　) overseas.

Exercise 3 日本文を英語に直しなさい。
音楽の潜在的な可能性について探るためにもっと研究が行われるべきです。

_____

Appendix

Grammar Points

Unit 1 5文型

(練習問題は 12 ページ)

▶ 英語の文は動詞を中心に成り立ち、構成要素の組み合わせによって5つの文型に分けられます。

第1文型	主語＋動詞（修飾語句を伴うことが多い。）	**Vegetables grew** in my garden.
第2文型	主語＋動詞＋補語（補語は名詞もしくは形容詞）（［主語＝補語］の関係が成り立つ）	**Growing vegetables is** not **easy**.
第3文型	主語＋動詞＋目的語（名詞もしくは代名詞など）	**He ate** fresh **vegetables**.
第4文型	主語＋動詞＋間接目的語［主に人］＋直接目的語［主に物］	**He gave me** some **vegetables**.
第5文型	主語＋動詞＋目的語＋補語（目的語＝補語の関係が成り立つ）	**He found gardening interesting**.

Unit 2 現在形・過去形

(練習問題は 16 ページ)

▶ 「動詞」が表す動作や状態がいつ起こったかという時間的概念は「動詞」の語形によって表します。

現在形	現在の事実	They **are** foreign tourists. A train **is** a popular vehicle.
	現在の習慣・反復的行為	I **go** to college by bus. / He often **travels** abroad.
	普遍的真理・ことわざ	Water **boils** at 100℃. / All roads **lead** to Rome.
	未来の代用	Please call me when you **arrive** there.
過去形	過去の動作・状態	We **traveled** to Britain last year. I **was** on the train at that time.
	過去の習慣・反復的行為	I **enjoyed** traveling to unfamiliar places. She seldom **traveled** by plane.

Unit 3 進行形・完了形

（練習問題は 20 ページ）

▶ 進行形「be 動詞 + ing」は限られた期間の間だけ進行する動作や状態を表します。

現在進行形	主語 + is/are + 現在分詞	I **am swimming** now.
過去進行形	主語 + was/were + 現在分詞	I **was swimming** when you called me.
未来進行形	主語 + will be + 現在分詞	The plane **will be landing** shortly.

▶ 完了形は「have/has/had + 過去分詞」は、時間軸上のある時点を基準として、その時点までの動作の完了、継続、経験、結果を表します。

現在完了	主語 + have/has + 過去分詞	I **have lived** here for 5 years.（継続）
過去完了	主語 + had + 過去分詞	I **had** never **fallen** in love before I met you.（経験）
未来完了	主語 + will have + 過去分詞	I **will have finished** the work by tomorrow.（完了）

* have been と have gone の違い

  He has been to Italy.（彼はイタリアに行ったことがある　経験）

  He has gone to Italy.（彼はイタリアに行ってしまった　結果）（今はここにいない）

Unit 4 助動詞

（練習問題は 24 ページ）

▶ 助動詞は動詞に未来、可能、推量などの意味を加える役割をします。

will	〜だろう（未来）	It **will** snow around Christmas.
	〜するつもりである（意志未来）	I'll invite you for Thanksgiving.
can	〜できる（可能）	We **can** have a BBQ in the park.
	（否定文で）〜のはずがない（否定推量）	That **cannot** be a ghost.
may	〜かもしれない（推量）	He **may** come to the party.
	〜してよい（許可）	**May** I unwrap the presents?
must	〜しなければならない（義務）	You **must** follow the rules.
	〜にちがいない（推量）	That story **must** be true.
	（否定文で）〜してはいけない（禁止）	You **must** not open the present.
should	〜すべきだ（義務）	You **should** try it.

Unit 5 受動態

(練習問題は 28 ページ)

▶ 能動態の文を受動態の文にするには、目的語 (O) を主語 (S) にし、動詞 (V) を「be ＋ 過去分詞」の形に変えて作ります。

能動態の文型	能動態	受動態
S V O	Some people **eat** various kinds of fish.	Various kinds of fish **are eaten** by some people.
S V O O	My mother **made** me French fries.	French fries **were made** for me by my mother.
S V O C	Music **keeps** me healthy.	I **am kept** healthy by music.

▶ 助動詞＋V原形の受動態は、「助動詞 ＋ be（の変化形）＋ 過去分詞」の形に変えます。

能動態	受動態
Many people **can eat** the special food.	The special food **can be eaten** by many people.
The chef **will send** me a menu.	A menu **will be sent** to me by the chef.

Unit 6 不定詞・動名詞

(練習問題は 32 ページ)

▶ 不定詞は「to ＋ 動詞の原形」で表され、文中の機能によって3つの用法があります。

名詞的用法	文の主語、目的語、補語になる	I want **to go** to America.
形容詞的用法	名詞/代名詞を後から修飾する	She needs something hot **to drink**.
副詞的用法	動詞・形容詞・副詞を修飾する	We went to the library **to study**.

＊ 原形不定詞とは「to のつかない不定詞」で、知覚動詞（see, hear, feel）や使役動詞（make, have, let）などと一緒に使用されます。
　　I saw her leave the room.（私は彼が部屋から出て行くのを見た）
　　Please let me know.（私にお知らせ下さい）

▶ 動名詞は「動詞＋ing」で表され、通常の名詞と同じく文の主語・目的語・補語になります。
▶ 不定詞は「to ＋ 動詞の原形」で表され、文中の機能によって3つの用法があります。

＊ 動名詞は前置詞の目的語としても使われます。

▶ 動名詞だけを目的語にとる動詞　finish, enjoy, mind, avoid, give up, postpone, escape　など
▶ 不定詞だけを目的語にとる動詞　want, learn, hope, expect, manage, pretend, promise　など

Unit 7 名詞・代名詞 （練習問題は 36 ページ）

▶ 名詞には数えられる名詞（可算名詞）と数えられない名詞（不可算名詞：advice, homework, furniture など）があります。

可算名詞	単数形（a ～ /an ～） 複数形（～ s/ ～ es）	I have a **class** today. He has three **classes** today.
不可算名詞	water, the water, some water, a glass of ～などを用いて数えます	I want some **water**, please. Give him a glass of **water**.

▶ 代名詞は名詞の代わりに用いられます。前に出た名詞の繰り返しを避けるために使われます。
　　I am taking a math class. **It** (=The math class) is very interesting.

Unit 8 形容詞・副詞 （練習問題は 40 ページ）

▶ 形容詞には直接名詞を修飾する限定用法と動詞の補語として用いられる叙述用法があります。

限定用法	名詞が表す意味の範囲を限定する	I saw a **blue** moon last night.
叙述用法	主語や目的語の名詞の状態・性質を叙述する	The water tastes a little **salty**.

* present, certain, late など、限定用法と叙述用法で意味が異なる形容詞もあります。
* asleep, alive など叙述用法のみの形容詞、elder, former など限定用法のみの形容詞にも注意。
* large population, strong coffee など、形容詞と名詞のコロケーションにも注意。
* necessary, possible, convenient など人が主語にならない形容詞もあります。
　　It is necessary for you to write a paper on physics. (× You are necessary to write …)

▶ 副詞は動詞、形容詞、副詞、文全体など様々なものを修飾します。
　　[動詞を修飾]　　　　　He has been studying chemistry **hard** since he entered high school.〈様態〉
　　[形容詞・副詞を修飾]　A **very** bright star can be seen **fairly** well from here.〈程度〉
　　[文全体を修飾]　　　**Luckily**, we had a chance to see the solar eclipse last month.〈話者の気持ち〉

Appendix

Unit 9 前置詞

(練習問題は 44 ページ)

▶ 前置詞は名詞・代名詞の前に置かれ、名詞や動詞を修飾する句を作ります。

at	時の一点（**at** 4 p.m.）／場所の一点（**at** the corner）
in	時間の中（**in** the evening）／空間の中（**in** the house）／手段（**in** Japanese）
on	曜日（**on** Sunday）／日付（**on** June 14）／接触（**on** the ceiling）
for	継続期間（**for** two weeks）／方向（**for** Tokyo）／理由（**for** this reason）
by	期限（**by** the deadline）／近接（**by** my side）／手段（**by** taxi）
until	継続の終了点（**until** [**till**] next week）

＊ because of や in spite of などのように2語以上で前置詞の役割を果たすものもあります。

Unit 10 接続詞

(練習問題は 48 ページ)

▶ 接続詞には文法上対等関係にある語・句・節をつなぐ等位接続詞と、主節と従属節をつなぐ従位接続詞があります。

等位接続詞	語/句/節＋接続詞＋語/句/節	I quit smoking, **and** I am healthy now.
従位接続詞	主節＋接続詞＋従属節	I quit smoking **because** the doctor told me to.

＊ 等位接続詞：and, or, but, so, for など
＊ 従位接続詞（名詞節を導く）：that, if, whether など（従属節は主語・目的語・前の名詞と同格などの働きをする）
＊ 従位接続詞（時の副詞節を導く）：when, as, while など（while は対比、as は比例・理由・譲歩の意味もあります）
＊ 従位接続詞（条件の副詞節を導く）：if, unless, once など
＊ 従位接続詞（譲歩の副詞節を導く）：though, although, whether など
＊ 従位接続詞（理由の副詞節を導く）：because, since など

▶ both A and B, either A or B, so 形容詞・副詞 that のように2語で成り立つ接続詞もあります。

Unit 11 比較

（練習問題は 52 ページ）

▶ 2つを比べる場合比較級を、3つ以上を比べる場合最上級を使います。

比較級	最上級
形容詞、副詞＋er または more ＋形容詞、副詞	the ＋形容詞、副詞＋est または the ＋ most ＋形容詞、副詞
音節の少ない語（big（1音節）early（2音節）） 音節の多い語（beautiful（3音節））	〜 er, the 〜 est more 〜 , the most 〜
My dog is bigger than yours.	He is the **tallest** in the soccer team.
The actress is more beautiful than her.	This is the **most difficult** problem in life.
This train runs faster than the bus.	She arrived home the **earliest** among family members.

Unit 12 関係代名詞

（練習問題は 56 ページ）

▶ 関係代名詞は接続詞と代名詞の機能をあわせ持ち、2つの文を1つにまとめることができます。
▶ 関係代名詞は先行詞の種類や関係節内での文法的機能によっていくつかの種類があります。

先行詞の種類	主格	所有格	目的格
人	who	whose	who / (whom)
人以外	which	whose	which

＊ 主格と目的格の関係代名詞は that で代用できます（ただし、先行詞に最上級や only などの強調表現が含まれる場合は that が優先されます）。目的格の関係代名詞は省略されることが多く、特に口語ではこの傾向が顕著です。

▶ what は先行詞を含む関係代名詞で the thing(s) which, anything that などの意味で用いられ、文の主語・目的語・補語となる名詞節を導きます。

  What (= The thing which) you need most is some rest.
  I will do **what** (= anything that) I can do.

▶ 先行詞の意味を限定する用法を制限用法、先行詞についての追加的な説明をする用法を非制限用法と呼びます。

  I have two sons who became doctors.（息子が他にもいる含意がある）
  I have two sons, who became doctors.（息子は2人のみである）

Unit 13 関係副詞

(練習問題は 60 ページ)

▶ 関係副詞とは接続詞と副詞の機能を持つ語で、先行詞の表す内容により 4 種類あります。

先行詞	関係副詞	例文
時	when	I remember the day **when** you won the award.
場所	where	This is the school **where** I studied.
理由	why	Explain the reason **why** you passed the exam.
方法	how	Explain **how** you passed the exam.

* 関係副詞を使った文で先行詞が当然わかる場合、先行詞を省略できます。

I know (the place) where we got together. I know (the time) when we should get together.

* 方法を表す how の場合、先行詞 (the way) か関係副詞の両方を使うことはできません。

Explain the way you passed the exam. = Explain how you passed the exam.

Unit 14 仮定法

(練習問題は 64 ページ)

▶ 仮定法には、仮定法過去と仮定法過去完了の 2 種類があります。

仮定法過去	現在の事実に反する内容を仮定	If I **were** rich, I **could buy** an imported car. = I'm not rich. So I cannot buy an imported car. I wish I **were** a millionaire. = I'm not a millionaire.
仮定法過去完了	過去の事実に反する内容を仮定	If I **had been** rich, I **could have bought** an imported car. = I was not rich. It was impossible to buy an imported car. I wish I **had been** a millionaire. = I was not a millionaire.

* 仮定法の重要表現

1. as if 主語 + 動詞（過去）「あたかも〜のように」He speaks as if he were my boss.
2. If it were not for + 名詞（句）= But for + 名詞（句）= Without + 名詞（句）「〜がなければ」

   If it were not for water, we could not live.

大学英語教育学会 （JACET）
リスニング研究会

代表　　高　橋　寿　夫

執筆者　岩　井　麻　紀
　　　　梶　浦　眞由美
　　　　川　越　栄　子
　　　　神　野　雅　代
　　　　高　橋　寿　夫
　　　　松　村　優　子
　　　　米　崎　啓　和

著作権法上，無断複写・複製は禁じられています。

Power-Up College English <Basic>　　　　[NSS-22]
パワーアップ・イングリッシュ〈基礎編〉

1刷　2019年4月1日
4刷　2024年8月26日

著　者　JACETリスニング研究会

発行者　南雲一範　Kazunori Nagumo
発行所　株式会社　南雲堂
　　　　〒162-0801　東京都新宿区山吹町361
　　　　NAN'UN-DO Co., Ltd.
　　　　361 Yamabuki-cho, Shinjuku-ku, Tokyo 162-0801, Japan
　　　　振替口座：00160-0-46863
　　　　TEL: 03-3268-2311（営業部：学校関係）
　　　　　　　03-3268-2384（営業部：書店関係）
　　　　　　　03-3268-2387（編集部）
　　　　FAX: 03-3269-2486

編集者　加藤　敦

イラスト　パント 大吉

装　丁　Nスタジオ

組　版　Office haru

検　印　省　略

コード　ISBN978-4-523-18522-2　C0082

Printed in Japan

E-mail　nanundo@post.email.ne.jp
URL　https://www.nanun-do.co.jp/